MARNEY

by Mary Kratt

Myers Park Baptist Church
1800 Queens Road
Charlotte, N. C.

For those who loved him
and some who didn't

Since memory is selective, Carlyle Marney was both more and less than is remembered here. These fragments of wide-ranging conversations represent only a small cross-section of those who knew him during his Charlotte years (1958-67). Marney lore is rich and endless and those who knew him are exceptional storytellers themselves. The story, of course, is far from ended.

For the purpose of this book, the letters, tapes, and notes of long conversations were edited consistently for clarity and brevity.

Grateful acknowledgement is given to Elizabeth Marney for her gracious assistance;

to Gene Owens who originated this project and secured a publication grant from the Endowment Fund;

to the Knight Publishing Company for photographs and information;

to Abingdon Press for permission to reprint excerpts from Carlyle Marney's books: BEGGARS IN VELVET (1960), STRUCTURES OF PREJUDICE (1961), THE RECOVERY OF THE PERSON (1963);

and to fifty generous persons listed on the final page of this book, for their stories, assistance, and encouragement.

Introduction

The second Senior Minister of the Myers Park Baptist Church (1958-67) was a Tennessee mountain man with only one name—Marney.

For ten years he fermented in Texas before he came to the Park. He swaggered in, ("didn't want to come," my foot!) trailing mud and horse manure, speaking a language few understood, swapping yarns around sophisticated camp fires, living and preaching a Gospel of tough freedom. God, he drawled, is a wild mustang, kicking the slats out of every man-made corral and running off into the world. And if God's keepers, herders, people intend to throw him down and place their brand on him, they are in for a disappointing round-up. But, if they want to tag along with this wild one, they can become pilgrims and wanderers.

At Myers Park Baptist, Marney found some Christians who were willing to be "messed with"; and the messing around was mutual. He thrived on it. Abandon your fourth grade Sunday School religion—that was his challenge. Take a leap of faith. Risk! Marney led the way—always risking. Every time he caught a fish, he cut it up for bait and went for something bigger. Risked little truths for Truth. Open, always, for new light to break through. What a tantalizing, threatening faith-pilgrimage. How exhilarating and frustrating and faithful for people and preacher. Church grew from it. Exercised muscles, developed fiber.

Relationship between this pastor and this congregation was a marvel. From a distance it was viewed with a hopefulness that was saving. If a people could live with such a character as Marney. . . . If an expansive person like Marney could exercise his kind of ministry with a local congregation. . . . If such could be, and was, then there was hope for fledgling clergy yearning to be free in ministry. What a gift to Church from Marney and Myers Park Baptists!

Upon coming as Senior Minister to Myers Park, I told the Pulpit Search Committee that I would rather try to follow Jesus than to succeed Marney. It took the disciples a few years to organize and disseminate the stories of Jesus—Marney was living legend. I still have his first letter to me in that succession. He opened:

If all the churches should close down, I should still hold that Myers Park should stay open. I found there (and left there) the most Church I know. And, I learned there, from laity, more than all my work-prior had produced. So I am happy for you and for them.

Long ago I should have written—but how does one use words to communicate a great love-affair. This I must say: I can almost never be free to attend, but my membership and contributions remain there simply because there's no one else to join—for after Sinai, who wants another mountain?

Gene Owens

What do we, any of us, know of our friends and acquaintances save that on such and such a date we saw them and that they did or said this, that, or the other to which words and acts we witness.

Ezra Pound

THE CALL

Carlyle Marney didn't want to come.

After Dr. George Heaton, Myers Park Baptist's first pastor, resigned in 1957 to become a full-time industrial counselor, Lex and Betty Marsh were asked to look in on Marney at the First Baptist Church in Austin, Texas.

Marney was impressive, but clearly uninterested. Why had they bothered?

The pulpit committee knew early that a search for a liberal Baptist of exceptional stature would require a wide net. In Montreat Lib Dowd asked for suggestions from James McCord (current president of Princeton Theological Seminary) who was then dean of Austin Presbyterian Theological Seminary,

Without hesitation, he considered Marney, ecumenically speaking, the greatest preacher in the Southeast. Marney was on his faculty as Professor of Christian Ethics.

T. J. Norman came back from his source,

I was given the assignment of visiting Dr. Robert McCracken, who was at that time the senior minister of Riverside Church in New York. He was a very distinguished man in the pulpit. I went with a long list of men we were thinking about. As we went through the list, he shared his own knowledge of them. He wanted to know what we knew about Marney. I indicated that "vibes were good as far as we were concerned." He said, "Well you can't get him." We talked about some other men. As the day went on, McCracken said, "Well, Marney is your man, but you can't get him." McCracken knew a little about our church and some of the people. He held Marney in very high regard.

Fred Helms' son-in-law, Joe Tyson, a student at Union Theological Seminary in New York insisted,

Why don't you folks get Carlyle Marney?

Helms had never heard of Marney. Tyson described him, sent Marney's book FAITH IN CONFLICT to Helms, who recalls Lib Dowd's report from McCord. McCord told her the man to get was Carlyle Marney,

But if he undertakes to leave Austin, I'll break both of his legs.

Lex Marsh recalls,

Nobody had interviewed him. I was asked to go to his church, hear him at morning service, make an appointment for that afternoon and tell him frankly we were looking for a preacher. He was very nice about it. "This is very interesting, but before we go any further in this conversation, I want you to know the last thing I'm interested in is a job. I am so well fixed here that I just couldn't walk away. I'm with a group of people who have accepted me in their hearts. I have developed some very fast and wonderful relationships. In my church I've got the heirarchy of the political structure of Texas and several members of my church have been governors of Texas or have been leading candidates for the job. Of course there are a lot of Baptists in Texas and half the politicians living around here are Baptists, and about half of them are members of my church. I've got the greatest forum in the world and this is just too good to terminate.

"Also, I've got two horses that I'm terribly fond of. I couldn't keep them inside the city."

I said, "Dr. Marney, that's perfectly all right. I can solve that problem. I live just a couple of miles from the church, but I've got horses myself. It just so happens that I've got six stalls in my barn and only two horses. I will take care of your horses." And Marney added, "Really, I just can't seriously negotiate."

When Marney was finally persuaded to visit Charlotte, T. J. Norman remembers clearly,

Rush Dickson chewed on and smoked more cigars that day than most days. Rush was pretty frustrated. He was used to having his own way about a lot of things. With the use of some four-letter words he said, "If you weren't so big, I'd pick you up and toss you right out this window." We saw that here was the man that we wanted, but every time we approached him, he would beautifully and skillfully rebuff us. We didn't get anywhere that afternoon, but that evening there seemed to be some hope. We finally wore each other out.

Fred Helms recalls,

Rush Dickson got so mad, he said, "Well, dammit, if that's the way you feel, you ought to go back and stay in Austin the rest of your life."

Lib Dowd quotes Rush Dickson's gripping Marney by his lapels, looking him straight in the eye,

We want you lock, stock and barrel.

This story has numerous articulate versions, all attesting to Dickson's straightforward approach and colorful language.

Lake Dickson (Rush's widow) tells it,

Marney told me he had heard this was a country club church and he didn't want to come. Rush, visiting him before he came here, got him by the tie, "You son-of-a-bitch, come!"

Marney in a 1976 interview with Bill Finger, described the incident himself:

After six months of discussion I had not found an issue on which I agreed with the chairman of the committee selecting the new pastor. Finally, after three days of talking, he took me by the tie and said "Damn you, you're the meanest man to talk a little religious business with I ever saw. There's nothing we agree on. If I did what I want to do, I'd throw you out this seventh-story window and forget you. But are you willing to be my pastor?" And I said, "I'd love to be your pastor." And that settled it.

It is strong testimony to Marney's personality and their own sense of adventure that the pulpit committee voted to recommend calling him. Marney came to meet all fifty of them, waiting stalwart and hopeful, gathered at the church. To the interview Marney wore a white linen suit, white shoes, and a black string tie. One member recalls, "He looked like a traveling evangelist."

Lex Marsh has no doubts about why Marney accepted the call:

It was easy to see that this was an opportunity that might match up with the one he had in Texas. He had been there eleven years. His family was in Tennessee not too far away. Much closer than Texas.

Bob Bryant believes,

He came because he probably thought, "Hell, maybe this crowd's worth messin' with."

And Fred Helms is just as certain,

When Marney came here, I think he was moving and didn't know why. He said from the pulpit he didn't want to come.

THAT MAN MARNEY

And when he came, the myths preceded him. He was a character from the very beginning because of his appearance and no less, of course, because of those things he said.

Some of his first words quoted in Charlotte were from those from his farewell to his Texas Church:

Anybody can come to Texas without anyone knowing, but you can't leave without committing a breach of the peace.

Many Austin Presbyterians congratulated me on my coming to their Mecca—Charlotte. I was a member of the faculty of the Presbyterian Seminary in Austin, but I don't think that's why they haven't grown more theologians. I did the best I could.

I have been put under a kind of spiritual arrest from within to serve the same cause for the same purpose in another city. The Myers Park Church reflects also the power and the presence of the great church to which we all belong.

Church members look back on those early days and remember:

Marney looked bigger than he actually was, like a great big guy even though he was only about six feet. He had a manner that was very commanding.

—T. J. NORMAN

I remember his first sermon. I had never seen him before, but I remember his stepping into the pulpit. . . . His hair was still red and he was a completely and totally unexpected, different type of preacher. As I remember, his first sermon was, "Here I am and let me tell you a little bit about where I think we can be and go." You knew you were in the presence of someone who had an extra gift.

—STUART DICKSON

When Marney came, I was teaching adult Sunday School. The first time he was available, we invited him to our class to a party. I looked forward as teacher to being honored by him. The first statement he made to the class was, "You got too many people in there. Too many is what you got." Here I stood thinking I would get praise from Carlyle Marney. Nothing like that at all.

George Heaton knew us all, knew our families. Here comes his successor and says, "I have not come to hold your hands. Even when you are in the hospital, I don't know whether I'm coming to see you."

—ARNO HART

Marney had a Thursday morning class of women, most of them Presbyterians. Rush said he guessed "Presbyterians are more used to education than Baptists." Marney did this class yearly, stopped teaching each spring and said to us, "You need to go out in your yards and work." He probably had things he wanted to do too.

Rush thought Marney was a man's man. Rush and Marney didn't agree on much, but they loved each other.

—Lake Dickson

Marney was not just a man's man. He put on an exterior that was rough as pig iron. Innately he was very sentimental. He was brusque at times and he had no thought of holding hands for these superannuated ladies in the congregation who wanted somebody to hold their hands because they didn't have anything else to do. He was not interested in that.

When he first came here, he had Sunday afternoon conferences which were attended by large crowds, many more non-members than members. He never dodged a question. It didn't make any difference what the question was, whether it was history, philosophy or theology, literature, art, no question ever stumped him.

—Fred Helms

Marney could speak to anybody. This was one of the amazing things about him. Near the first night in Austin [when Jim Berry came from Westminster Choir College to work for Marney as choir director], Marney came by and wanted to take me out to a meeting where he was preaching. This turned out to be just an old brush arbor, way out in the edge of the hill country, a cross-roads Baptist church with a bunch of cowboys. He wanted me to hear their booster band sing . . . to indoctrinate me into the church music of Texas. Those children got up there and yelled, "If the devil don't like it, he can sit on a tack." I began to wonder, but it was fun.

He was the kind of person who said, "Now that you're the Minister of Music, that's your job and I don't want to have anything to do with it. I expect you to do it the best you can, I'm not going to get in your way." And he didn't. . . . I did a Heinrich Schutz Christmas Cantata and it was hard . . . Marney said, "You know, if you get too far ahead of your folks, they mistake you for the enemy and start shooting."

In Charlotte just the routine of working with the divided chancel was different. In Austin it was very simple because Marney and I were back to back and all he had to do on the invitation hymn was punch me or look at me and that was the end of the hymn. We didn't sing "amens" in Austin. Here we did. One of our first Sundays at Myers Park Marney turned round to me and mouthed something I didn't quite read. What he was trying to say was, "Sing the amen." I thought he said, "This is the end." I signalled the choir and we stopped. Dr. Marney was standing right out in front of the chancel alone. He started out with an "A . . ." facing the congregation, and turned around and ended on 'men' facing me. Dragging it out all by himself, he turned to the congregation and said, "Well, you want to laugh, why don't you?"

Something I'll always remember is Marney's beautiful voice. Every Wednesday in Austin he would, in a study of the book of Acts, for instance, stand with the Bible in his hands and read. He would explain and talk about it. I used to sit on the front pew and watch how he shaped those words. He could sing too. One time I got in late and he had already started them singing. In fact, when he was in school in Tennessee, he led the music in revivals playing the trombone.

—JAMES A. BERRY

When I heard Marney was coming . . . , I tried to read everything he had done. I thought when I met him I would impress him by knowing some things about him. So I did.

When I saw him I thought he was impressive and I liked him from the very beginning, was very much awed by him. I told him that I enjoyed reading one particular book. He told me that book wasn't for teenagers. I enjoyed his humor because he picked me up probably as a victim . . . picking me out to carry on some needling. That was the way it was. I was constantly shot down and thinking I was going to come up the next time on top.

I invited them to dinner at our house. I was going to put on the dog for the new minister. I had beef stroganoff . . . Bob's mother and father had sent the man who came every now and then when they had big company to help in the kitchen, and I was really making a very big impression. We went to the door to greet them and Marney turned to Elizabeth and said, "Elizabeth, what did you say her name was?" He did it again. It started right there, the kind of friendship was set up, for he was one up all the time.

He said later that he never was crazy about beef stroganoff and he also realized that was not exactly the way we ate every day. We had a lot of laughs over that Big Evening . . . I thought it was going to be impressive and I found out he wasn't that kind of impressive. You didn't bother to impress Marney, you didn't need to, he really didn't care. I always felt a kindred spirit with him.

Bob said I had a personal relationship with him before he did. He thought Marney stood off with him, and I think he did. Then they resolved that after a couple of years. It turned out it was because Bob was a funeral director. He told Bob why later. Bob didn't match up, the person he was and being a funeral director. He didn't have to get in his say. But it took a while before this really got resolved.

. . . Marney was afraid to let people know how sensitive he was a lot of times. I don't think he ever knew how to say "no" or how to sort out his priorities for himself or for meeting the needs of other people . . . I never saw him when he wasn't serious about somebody's hurting. I never saw him put anybody down . . . in the beginning I thought he was putting me down. It wasn't that at all. Marney had a way of jibbing and jabbing that was sort of sharp, but if you really got to know him, you knew he really felt sensitive to other people's feelings.

He appreciated things in people that were unusual too . . . He collected characters all the time. He admitted to that. Well, he was a character himself and he attracted people who were strange and odd.

I think one of his favorite characters he had and loved was Sam Buchlender, called him his personal Jew. Sam's dead now. He was a radical. He had suffered through the holocaust in Germany and had escaped there and gone to Cuba, then escaped from there. He was a philosopher, a short, stocky man with great big brown eyes. Just as bull-headed as Marney about his beliefs and thinking. They would lock horns, but Marney was always saying he learned from Sam.

—Sarah Bryant

The first time I was ever in the Marneys' house for a meal my sister who lives in Jacksonville was here and they invited us out for dinner. She told a fairly disreputable joke about a town in Texas called Waxahachie. Marney literally fell out of his chair laughing, just fell over on the floor. He was just that kind of person.

He wasn't prissy about what he said. He liked to joke as well as anybody . . . a towering intellect, but earthy . . . that kind of person who is not so far up in the ivory tower that you cannot reach him.

Marney didn't care a thing about convention. Not clothes, proper manners or anything. I remember that time we went off in the car to the mountains he had on white buckskin shoes and Elizabeth Marney said, "Nobody wears white buckskin shoes but Marney and Pat Boone."

—Priscilla Upchurch

. . . a man who had a dog like Copper couldn't be all bad. Marney was very masculine, very sexy.

—Charleen Swansea

Marney told me one time that if he were allowed to take only one tenor to Heaven with him, he'd take me.

—SAM WILLIAMS

When Marney came, there were folks in the church who had gotten used to leaving right at the stroke of twelve on Sunday Morning. He told them, "If I'm through what I'm telling you, you'll get out at twelve. If I'm not, you'll stay here til I get through."

He hated paperwork and detail. I worked for him as secretary about two years and he never did just one letter. He let the work set up for six weeks, then brought it all out at once.

He told me that his book about teenagers, DANGEROUS FATHERS, PROBLEM MOTHERS AND TERRIBLE TEENS, *taken from transcripts of a Texas television program, had sold the most copies. But the book he was proudest of was* STRUCTURES OF PREJUDICE.

All those books he wrote, we're in there.

—RAMELLE HOBBS

I had been interviewed here for a job with Bill Schwantes and he said I was qualified, but I would have to meet Dr. Marney before I could be hired. I came in one day and was sitting in the chair at the entry to the office, next to where Ramelle Hobbs was sitting.

A large man in blue jeans, dirty boots, and a cigarette hanging out of his mouth came in. I thought, "The poor man's come in to be counselled." And Ramelle said, "This is Dr. Marney." I was stunned. Where I was raised, as a Southern Baptist, a minister didn't go without a tie. I thought ministers slept in their collar and tie. After talking with him, I was still stunned.

He said, "We don't have a training union here. We don't have Wednesday night prayer meeting. Do you think we're going to hell?"

I said, "No, I guess not."

He said then, "Well, you'll fit in."

—GRACE PHIFER

Marney was especially vulnerable to characters who were down and out and didn't want to appear so. One Wednesday at staff meeting, Marney announced that after the meeting ended, the staff would all adjourn to the sanctuary where a former opera singer from Milan, Italy, who was now a voice coach, would give them lessons in voice projection. The man set up this machine in the center aisle. He ex-

plained when the speaker's voice projected sufficiently (which wasn't often), a red light would come on. For about a month the lessons continued and the young staff members would hear each other in the basement halls practicing the odd, booming exercises as we went on our regular church tasks. "Aaaaa-ommmmmm. Aaaaa-Ommmmmm." No one knows what happened to the opera singer (Marney didn't explain), but we remember Old Red Eye.

—Bob Howard

Marney was a man who believed in organization. When he came, he brought his team. He felt his job was to preach and other members of his staff had their jobs to do and he expected them to do them. At deacons' meetings he expected each man to get up and tell exactly what was being done in his field. If questions were asked, he turned to them, "You answer that." He expected them to perform. If someone didn't like what a staff member was doing, Marney would let them defend themselves in deacons' discussions, then he would get up and say, "Well, I stand behind so-and-so. But maybe some changes can be made." or "I'll look into it with this member." He wouldn't let it rest. He'd see it through, and come back at another meeting with an answer, or discuss it with the member.

—Dr. O. Hunter Jones

He was a workaholic.

—Haynes Baird
—T. J. Norman

He was utterly irrational about the use of his body and his time. It didn't make any sense the way he pushed himself, but that was his style.

I remember several of his favorite yarns, but I can't tell them on tape unfortunately. But there is another interesting thing about Marney. He was a puritan. He was in terms of his respect for women, his whole attitude toward sexuality; he had tremendous moral imperatives and feelings about this.

He was often criticized for his colorful language. But Marney was never profane. He could use colorful words, but they were always in a way germane to whatever the point he was discussing. He was never vulgar for the purpose of shock. He was a real puritan in terms of his demands on himself.

—Claude Broach

And an un-named parishioner described Marney to Kays Gary,

He's a guy who can follow you through a revolving door and come out first.

THE TRAVELING SHOW

It didn't take long to notice that Marney was entering a period of national ministry and carrying Myers Park Baptist right along with him. They were glad to ride his coattails or have him ride theirs. Whichever, it was a pleasureable and provocative journey.

Marney accepted invitations to speak and preach widely during his years at Myers Park: Princeton, Yale, Duke, the University of Chicago, Cornell, Harvard, West Point, Union (N.Y.), Riverside Church (N.Y.), the Far East Air Forces, Annapolis, and numerous others.

The fact that Marney consistently refused to fly made these trips longer than usual, but not many members complained. Sharing Marney with Yale, for instance, seemed to be worth doing.

The Board of Deacons had approved Marney's traveling and preaching away. It was not a problem.

—BOB BRYANT

Others did protest his absences. Priscilla Upchurch comments, *Any church you go to there is always a problem with a group of people. They wanted him to stay here. I remember Marney said, "You can easily get a dozen preachers who will stay all the time." A man who has something like Marney is asked to go places."*

On May 24, 1964 Marney and Archie Carroll, Myers Park Baptist layman, discussed changing church roles of laymen and clergy on CBS television's "Look Up and Live." It was a question-answer exchange with another pair of churchmen, Dr. Rubin Youngdahl, pastor of Mt. Olivet Lutheran, Minneapolis, Minn. and layman, Dr. Arnie Rydland. Chalmers Dale, program producer, referred to Youngdahl and Rydland as "an organizer and administrator, while Marney does things on a very personal level."

Archie Carroll recalls:

Before I accepted the invitation to go and do the program with Marney, I had a chat with him and I said, "Look, I don't know how you feel about it, but if I am supposed to say certain things or act in a certain way about my feelings of Christianity or being a member of a church, then you don't want me to go with you." You know Marney! That was what he wanted. I had no instructions. He wouldn't have taken anybody's instructions.

Gibby and I and Elizabeth and Marney together went up on the train and stayed at the Belvedere Hotel. At the CBS studios in Rockefeller Center, we met the lady who influenced CBS to use

Marney for the program. They explained how the time was set up to try to illustrate the different approaches to ministry. Dr. Youngdahl was minister of one of the largest churches in the nation, and organized to the hilt. Marney was a minister of a church that a lot of people think had a great deal of programming, but he wasn't all that programmed and organized. He was intensely relational. He believed that every layman in the church, if he is a genuine Christian, is himself a minister. This contrasts with the type of church hierarchy where the dictatorial powers of the pastor or minister say what will be done and who will do this and that. This pastor is a great salesman and overpowerer of his congregation. These are the two contrasting extremes. Very refreshing to see that demonstration in the CBS program. I wouldn't have taken anything for having participated in it.

The CBS program showed Marney's intense conception of ministry built around relationship, openness, and, honesty. He deplored sham, rigidity, and self delusion; hated those things with a passion.

Marney was very, very pleased at the way the program was put on and the way our comments were received by viewers. He was completely satisfied that our side won.

But it was another national television event that brought the clash of controversy Marney found delicious.

Christmas Eve, 1965, CBS brought its cameras to Myers Park Baptist's overflowing sanctuary for a nationally televised midnight Christmas sermon.

Most of all I remember the Christmas Eve when Marney was carried live on television from our church sanctuary. How proud I was. So I went to my friends like T. B. Wilkin in Blacksburg, S. C. "T. B., did you see Carlyle Marney? Did you see?"

He said, "Yes, and I did not understand a word he said."

—ARNO HART

I was astounded at the sermon he preached. Here was a national network zeroing in on a relatively small community and a Baptist church in the south, looking for a traditional type of Christmas service, an ecumenical service for the nation as a whole, and he came out of a box like a thoroughbred at a racetrack, shook the world up with a totally unexpected type of sermon. No roses. There was a lot of flak about it. There always is when someone's on the leading edge. He had a great capacity to make anyone think.

—STUART DICKSON

The church received more than 500 letters of praise and outrage. The praise outweighed the blame, but the recoil was potent. One irate letter called the sermon "a blasphemous substitute for what Baptists have traditionally believed and preached."

The Charlotte newspapers received and printed so many letters that on January 13, 1966 the Charlotte News reprinted the sermon in its entirety. Excerpts from that controversial sermon:

In a world where so many gods have lived too long; in a world where so many men have died senselessly and too soon; one grows diffident about all this god-death business. In a world with so many gods to spare who will miss another or two? Except that not even our false gods die. They wait around off-stage for another chance to get in on the act—then they come up on us from the rear.

We are here, I am sure, with a hunger born of some great wish—the wish to believe, or at least to be capable again of belief, or the wish to hear some authentic word. Our private wars consume us. . . . All of our buckets leak. . . .

If there is no way to peace from where we are with what we've got we have to make a very costly choice—for there is no peace with any lesser god still in our pack-sack. This means no peace and property; no peace and patriotism; no peace and position, no peace and power. It means no peace and any other priority. It means that even partial peace requires the release by us of some property, patriotism, position, and power. For these are the spoils of a war we have fought. . . .

Look backward. The last time you were at peace you were nine years old; pre-puberty, pre-property, pre-responsibility—except that you were already at war, with your brothers and your tribe and your treasures. Where is Peace? Nowhere—Erewhon! We shall have to live with War or without anything else unless there is either a new kind of peace or a new kind of man.

When God talked Peace once he did it by, with, and through a Man, the Only Man, the Man none of our wants and desires could entrap and enslave. There is no way to talk of true Peace until we have talked of true Manliness; and peace, whenever, comes over your shoulder and up from the rear.

The Star of this Hope is a man who weighs as much naked as dressed. He transcends the racial, regional, religious buckets of our existence by his ability to move in and out. He has dimensions of self-hood beyond nation, beyond property, beyond regional views of race. He knows that for everybody there is something more to be than American, white, Protestant, and local. There is a larger race, the human race. There is a larger region. There is a larger Church than ours. It is larger than all our protestant splitness; wider than our Roman Catholic-Greek Orthodox-Protestant separations. I speak of a truer Ecumenism within which a man knows that at bottom and at Source the Jew, the Christian, and the Muslim (all 700,000,000 plus of him) take their rise from the same high cry with which this service began—

Hear, O Israel, the Lord our God is One. . . .

And more: he must remember that Incarnation and all our cultural treasures and most tools came from even farther East at first, and that all exist for all the Sons of earth. Here only does,

> *"The Kingdom of this world . . . become*
> *The Kingdom of our Lord and of his Christ . . ."*

For such a man risk, danger, and anxiety are still implicit.

In all our modern moods and ways, I keep the terrible feeling that we have been over this reeking, smoky ground before this. It is too much to expect that our dreadful acedia can be reversed from here. But from a Church like this in size and shape, located in a Southern province of an empire, there once went out a Word of a Way that was the best we could hear for a thousand years.

So mought it be—again. If we knew what to say. This much of it we know; the stage, and the game, are bigger than we thought; all our "little boxes, little boxes" of race and national interest and temporary value hold only games not worth our lives. We have tools, unused tools, new tools in our hands, that can be used to transform these games we play into a drama of redemption. The new light which is breaking into our lives and work can show us a potential for this earth of which we have hardly dared dream. And,

One has gone before us into a Manhood and a Community that lies within our reach. The method is dialogical and requires us to hear each other. The setting is cruciform and demands our lives and fortunes. The characters are human. The drama has consequence—we can afford to work at being brothers to the race because we have met here, and there, too, a very great Grace.

And after the smoke had cleared, Marney answered a letter from the President of the area broadcasting affiliate that carried the program:

February 24, 1966

Dear Charlie Crutchfield:

. . . I am moved by your discerning insight that controversy is essential. We are learning in Adult Education at our place that nothing happens before disagreement.

It is now two months since our Christmas Eve Service. I still have daily some mail or other from that hour. . . . From friends in New York City I heard that all the CBS brass stayed up for this one to see if Pamela had pulled one green—but their opinion was that it was their best since the beginning ten years ago. So—we have cause to be glad. Of course, anytime the press debates for seven weeks whether it was even a sermon or not—I think maybe it was.

Regards

Marney

Mr. Charles Crutchfield
WBT, One Julian Price Place
Charlotte, North Carolina

PREACHING THE GOSPEL ACCORDING TO MARNEY

A preacher who doesn't stretch you is no good.

—CARLYLE MARNEY

Marney attracted admirers and sermon tasters from all denominations. They appeared wherever and whenever he preached. The pews at Myers Park always contained visitors who came "to hear Marney" and who later, if asked what he had said, found themselves hard put to explain, let alone summarize. No one denied, however, that he was extraordinary.

It must also be noted that there were some church members who hated him, who refused to attend worship or contribute money "as long as that communist is there."

Marney didn't blink an eye. He had told Lake Dickson about one of his first churches, a little church up in West Virginia with "the meanest people he had ever known. God laughed at me one night and said, 'You preach the truth and leave the rest to me.' I've been doing it ever since."

Marney had been promised a free pulpit when he was called. Fred Helms remembers:

Marney said time and time again that he never asked for a freer pulpit than this one. Nobody ever told him what he could do or what he couldn't do, what he could say or couldn't say, what he should preach or what he couldn't preach.

Marney told Priscilla Upchurch, "I feel that fifteen percent of the ministers in churches, particularly big city churches, don't preach what they believe. They are scared to lose their jobs."

Marney told Bill Finger in an interview that within three months after he came to Myers Park, Rush Dickson

—was going around to the folks who were already dissident and saying something like this: "You don't like what he's saying, do you? I despise it too, but I'll tell you what I'll do. There are 120 Baptist churches in this city. You pick one. And I'll pick up the balance of your pledge for the rest of this year. I'm going to stay." Now you can't buy that kind of power. That has to be given.

I had freedom at the Myers Park Church. And I enjoyed it. You could stand up there and whambang! It was a classic and beautiful place to preach. No, I didn't really have power, but I did pick up some sense.

In 1962 Marney was quoted, "I have had for 15 years a place where a man is free to say anything he wants to say, but he must not expect anybody to do anything about it." Perhaps some who professed not to understand Marney's erudition did not want to understand an uncomfortable message.

Divergent opinions have long been characteristic of Baptists. Assessments of Marney's preaching are no exception.

A lot of times I couldn't understand his sermons. People often got lost in his rhetoric, his amazing command of words. While he was here, I think he hit his preaching prime. It was the time of his life.

—BOB BRYANT

Early in the game, before I had learned to feel with Marney as well as think with him, before I began to allow myself to be carried along by his impressionistic style of preaching, I would frequently not understand him at all, or misunderstand a considerable amount of what he was saying-painting.

On the Monday following such a Sunday, I said to him, "Marney, I didn't understand what you were saying yesterday. It was miles above my head." To which he replied, "Well, McClernon, I guess that means that you're going to have to sit and stand and think and feel a little taller, doesn't it?" . . . He always knew we were capable of more.

—REV. BOB MCCLERNON

About half way in his time here people were always saying that he was too good to stay here and that somebody else would get him. . . .

The best thing about him was his intellectual approach to religion. . . . He had it on a plane I appreciate. People said they couldn't understand him. He loved history and he would start out and give a background of what he was going to say, way back yonder, Greek history, Roman history. It was real history to start with. I remember him talking about Taraboleum like in Greece, in Mary Renault's THE KING MUST DIE, *describing the ceremony where they had the bull upon the lattice and they would slit his throat and the blood would run down through these slats onto the person. That was the baptism of blood. I've heard people say, 'Why do I want to learn about that? That's not preaching the Gospel.' But that's what he did. And then he would go on and use it in a perfectly marvelous way to bring you a message that would really stick to your ribs. People quit listening. They would think 'what do I want to know about Taraboleum' and they wouldn't get the meat of what he was talking about.*

Marney's great good friend, Dr. James McCord, president of

Princeton Theological Seminary, said that Marney coming up to the pulpit looked like a whale rising from the sea. . . . People don't realize that to get up a good sermon you have got to have something else besides looking out the window and enjoying nature. You have got to study. He was a great student, Marney was. Long time ago we thought we might sell this house. He came to look at it and said, 'You know, this room would be fine if you would build bookcases all the way around it.'

—PRISCILLA UPCHURCH

Fred Helms tells a story that reflects on Marney's study habits:

Dr. Syd Stealey was the first President of Southeastern Baptist Seminary, knew Marney there, and met him one night at an annual meeting of a club of ministerial students. Syd had been the club president and Marney was president. Syd, who didn't weigh over 125 or 140 and was keen as can be, met Marney in the corridor. Syd said to Marney, "You are a big fellow. You've got a big voice. If you get up and start using your big physique and your big voice and you haven't got anything to say, it would be a hell of a thing, wouldn't it?"

Marney said, "I've sat up many a night all night working and reading and trying on account of what that little devil threw at me."

A member came to Marney one morning after a worship service and said, "Marney, I didn't believe much that you said this morning."

Marney replied, "You believe the New Testament, don't you?" and walked away.

Marney didn't coddle anybody, he expected you to do your own homework. Dr. Sydnor Stealey told this story to a group in our church. He said, "When Marney was working on his doctorate, I gave him four books to read. It would have taken the average student a month to read them. Marney brought them back in a week. "You haven't read those books," I said.

He said, "Ask Me."

I did and he had.

—JOHN WAGSTER

I thought Marney was a real intellectual, one of the greatest readers I have ever known. When he read a book, he seemed to devour it instead of read it. He was well over my head and I think that was equally true with other members of the church, who didn't quite get the idea, even after he preached. One of the toughest jobs

I ever had (since I was a little bit closer to him the first two or three years of his ministry here) was when he asked me to read a manuscript and I decided after an hour of that thing that I was just completely incapable. He turned over two or three manuscripts in a period of five years. But, I went through the motions of trying to read them and I could sense the fact that his books would never be best sellers. They were just above and beyond the capacity of the typical reader. I told him just that, and he accepted it in good spirit. It was no great surprise to him. I don't know that he was really disappointed. I think, like every other author probably, he had dreams of putting out something that would go through several printings, and would be widely circulated and turn out to be popular. Elizabeth, his wife, heard him talking about it and she said, "It is no way to make a living." It might be a necessary part of one's ministry and of course anybody with any claim to intellectual status would feel like the authorship of a book is an incident to that status.

—Lex Marsh

Marney could certainly get beyond anybody in his learning. Sometimes to follow him in his thoughts you had to be with him and know what he was reading. . . . He was bookish. He lived for learning. I felt it was unfortunate that he never became a part of the faculty of some of the larger, more influential seminaries of this country. He told me that he had the opportunity to join them, and this was not what he wanted.

—Ed Echerd

Everybody thought he was a great preacher because they didn't understand him. I thought most of the time he didn't have his topic sentence where it ought to be. His was convoluted preaching.

—Charleen Swansea

I'd say Marney was a magnificient preacher. His sermons read well. . . . When you analyze the language, how eloquent the language is all the time, almost blank verse, how it moves with poetic imagery, image on image, phrase on phrase. The voice was a great asset too. But in terms of the impact of his preaching, I've always felt that Marney was a mystic, that he created moods. He never gave you one, two, three points. He created a mood and flung it up against the chancel wall and you were either in it or out of it. And if you were in the mood, you got the mood and felt it. You went away and you felt that something really happened in here. But if anybody said "what did he say?" you said, "I'll be damned if I know."

—Claude Broach

Leslie Crutchfield Tompkins remembers,

I had a good friend whom I had been talking to about C. S. Lewis and Tillich and some books I'd been reading. He said there was somebody he wanted me to meet. He made an appointment with Marney and he and his wife and I drove out there one night and sat in his study and this giant was sitting there surrounded by wall-to-wall, floor-to-ceiling books. I think the books probably impressed me as much as the man. I thought anybody who had digested all those books was really something. We just talked. I don't remember what we talked about. I was impressed. Then I began coming over here to church. The man who introduced me to him was not a member, just someone who was interested in him. I started coming every week. I was impressed with his voice. I don't think I have ever heard, before or since, a voice like that and I'm very prone to voices, so I was hypnotized. It was most sonorous, a very deep, rich, beautiful voice. I felt that his sermons were poems. His phrasing, his rhythms and his sort of chanting technique he had when he was listing things. He would fall into this chant and you would just sit there and it was almost like music, certain forms of music.

We talked about books and ideas and I also talked to him about personal problems a few times, but where we talked the most, I think, was in the area of books. I was fascinated with all these sorts of "paper-back theologians." I didn't get into anything too deep, but I would read Tillich's easier stuff, and I told him I was writing poetry and took my poems for children to him. He was very helpful with it. In fact he showed them to a publisher who was coming to town. He told me to bring my poems over and he would show the man my poems, which he did, and I thought that was wonderful. Nothing ever came of it, but he gave me some good criticisms really. Looking back on it, what he said about the poems was really sharp, and he seemed to appreciate poetry. I felt that he preached and lectured poetically. That was his natural style. I think it was deliberate. I think he knew that he had a great gift for it and he used it. I didn't like the name dropping. Each sermon would be packed with all these erudite, learned, in-vogue names of theologians and I thought that was a little excessive. I think you can get things across without dropping the names because we obviously had not read all those books. That bothered me a little bit. But I figured if I had that much of a gift, I'd probably be throwing the names around too.

I remember I wrote him a note when I first met him and began to read more and didn't know him very well, but was fascinated with him. I wrote him a note and I said that I felt like a spiritual leech, because I wanted to learn all these things from him, and I always have about whoever had things that I wanted. It happened to be him at that time. I used the term 'spiritual leech.' I felt like I was asking, you know, seeking things from him, and he wrote back to me. This is his letter:

May 6, 1960

Dear Leslie:

We are all "leeches"—and you have answered your own query. You are discovering how one must carve out his own spiritual dignity in a jungle and this is Church—and is composed of those with whom he finds this. I long ago welcomed you to my private Church! It has dozens of hungry members—and here one learns but has no superiors or inferiors—if he can hear. Buber has it right—"In the beginning is relation."

Cordially,

C. MARNEY

I read Marney's books too, but they were disappointing to me. They weren't near up to his speaking, I didn't think. It didn't come out as well as it did coming from him. I don't know why this was so. It was sort of like his name dropping. There were too many footnotes. When you read a beautiful paragraph and you would think, oh, . . . and then there was a footnote. It was somebody else. Some of his books are just back-to-back footnotes. I felt that he could have written beautiful stuff. I don't know why. I think maybe the last one I didn't read, but I read all the rest. They were just disappointing, compared to his pulpit style and his sermons. His delivery was magic. For me it really was. Too much so, really. The man was almost too much there and you forgot what he was driving at sometimes.

Yes, I think the voice was something he almost couldn't help, but he used the chanting. He would fall into this thing where he would say, "da,da,da,da," and it was almost primitive—like Vachel Lindsay. A hypnotic sort of chant and you really didn't even care what he was saying, it sounded so beautiful. He could have been saying "Do, Ray, Mi" or something. I didn't always understand him clearly. I did much more at the beginning of his time here or my exposure to him than I did toward the end. When he came back to visit on the Dickson Lectures or whatever it is he came back for, he would preach and I would say, 'Oh yeah, I had forgotten that style.' It would all come back. He still had that same style. Marneyism. I felt that he changed, that he became more obscure or contradictory. I don't know which it was. But he had something going on, his thought was ahead of me and I really couldn't keep up with it, or whether he really was more ambivalent about some things he was saying. It became more confusing to me, to listen to him.

And what was he saying in all this preaching? Of his thirteen published books, five are collected sermons which can be read for an abbreviated view. But if you ask people who were there, they will most likely speak of taking off masks with one another, or humanism, conflict, the pilgrimage of finding where you have come from and where you are *at*, priesting, learning what to discard from the past, openness, relationship, etc. Any ten listeners produce ten different answers. But occasionally a few lodged one sermon in their minds like a nugget.

It was the one he preached on graven images. I had grown up hearing about idols and reading about the golden calves—having nothing to grab on to in terms of understanding that, symbolically or any other way. I remember what Marney said about the graven images, that we make of the self a graven image. We have this self and we surround it with things that we think represent it. This can take the form of material things like big cars or fancy clothes or other things like our life style that seem to tell us who this self is. But, then we get all of these things with which we surround ourselves confused with the self and we begin to worship the symbols rather than the self and the symbols become carved substitutes, which is what he said a graven image is. That is where we start to lose track of who we are. That is what idolatry is. I remember that more than anything else that he preached.

—NANCY GEER

What I experienced most was that he called one forth to be somebody, not to lean against a post and wait like the Jews at the waters of Babylon for what is going to happen, but to find strength within my own self to put to use and to become.

—ARNO HART

THE LUNCH COUNTER ENCOUNTER GROUP

Character is the real race problem
—CARLYLE MARNEY, JULY 16, 1963

Unless we make the plight of the Negro American the central concern of all Americans, there will be no social peace in this generation to come.

A candid history of the South and its people would be unendurable for a Southerner to read. We could not face it. Shorn of its myths and legends we would repudiate it as not our own.

—Marney, December 6, 1965

Dr. Haynes Baird, Marney's good friend and frequent verbal adversary, recalls

Marney and I disagreed violently on the integration thing at times. Not on the basic issue, but on the methods by which it ought to be accomplished.

You have to admire him for being such an idealist. I remember one thing he said, "Haynes, you know I get this thing on me and it's like a stomach full of food and you've just got a terrific desire to have a bowel movement and you've got to get it off your mind." I think those were his exact words. He says, "I've got to get this across to people. I've got to put it in writing, get it out through my sermons. I've got to get them listening."

In April, 1963, when newspapers were filled with news of orbiting spacecraft and those winsome pictures of two year old John-John Kennedy toddling behind his father, the President, into the Oval Office, audible discontent rumbled in the South.

Public schools had been closed in Prince Edward County, Virginia, for four years rather than desegregate. The quiet prayer marchers in Birmingham, Alabama, in May began an effective economic squeeze by boycotting downtown merchants. Governor George Wallace declared at the University of Alabama on May 22, "I'll be present to bar the entrance of any Negro who attempts to enroll."

And in North Carolina during that same week of May 19, police arrested fifty persons in Durham protesting outside a Chinese restaurant, 250 picketed department stores in Fayetteville, fifty sang hymns in Wilmington streets picketing for equal employment and removal of segregated signs in public places. Marches began in Chapel Hill, High Point and on May 21, Johnson C. Smith University students in Charlotte marched quietly in columns of twos to the courthouse on the anniversary of the Mecklenburg Declaration of Independence.

Stan Brookshire, mayor of Charlotte at the time, remembers well,

the spring of 1963, May, June, and July, the Charlotte Community Relations Committee's effort to keep the peace. Dr. Marney and about six other ministers met with me to discuss it.

In the first meeting Dr. Marney said, "Well, let's don't worry too much about this matter. This is a human relations problem. In 3000 years from now, there'll be only one race, the human race."

On Sunday morning following the week of encroaching dissent, Buell Duncan, prominent businessman and Chamber of Commerce Director, spoke to Brookshire at the Myers Park United Methodist Church where they attend. He asked if Brookshire thought Ed Burnside, Chamber President, businessman and Myers Park Baptist deacon, would take some action in the desegregation matter.

Brookshire says,

I called Ed. Ed called an Executive Committee meeting that next morning. We didn't want what happened in Durham, Winston-Salem, Raleigh to happen—the marches at night, the people lying in the streets.

A committee of three wrote a resolution that the Chamber recommend businesses serving the public drop discrimination on the basis of race, creed or color.

The next day, May 24, Burnside conducted the meeting and the resolution was approved unanimously.

Burnside said afterwards,

We do not want to tell any man what to do or what not to do, we only wish to state what we think is right in principle.

Brookshire tells that,

Slug Claiborne, a Charlotte restaurateur, made the suggestion that white leaders take black leaders to hotel dining rooms by prior arrangement. He challenged the committee asking them to do this.

Arrangements were made in advance for Wednesday, Thursday, and Friday of that same week with the managements of the Manger, the Barringer, Hotel Charlotte and one or two others. The media agreed not to publicize it in advance. The pattern was for a pair of white leaders to take a pair of blacks. There were no incidents whatsoever.

And when Dr. Martin Luther King spoke at the Charlotte Coliseum a few days later (May 31) to the graduates of six local black high schools, he praised the Charlotte move to desegregate leading motels and hotels as "significant and meaningful."

Brookshire continues,

We still had the problem to convince the rest of the restaurants to admit others. Some didn't want to go along. But there were no problems. The hotels began admitting guests for meals and rooms. It took all summer and much footwork and conversations by Dr. John Cunningham's Community Relations Committee to desegregate the hotels, motels, and theaters. Theaters were more difficult.

There is no question that desegregation's happening here was a result of pressure. Pressure was being put on us, Durham, Winston-Salem, and it was getting close, threatening boycotts of businesses, buses. We acted because of social conscience, civic pride, and economics.

There is no claim here that Carlyle Marney had the crucial role in Charlotte's desegregation negotiations. Records and personal reports evidence a wide and careful community effort. But local power at that time lay in the Chamber of Commerce. It is significant to note in the interpretations of persons and the sequence of events, the point at which power was effectively exerted.

Marney was not a rabid advocate of integration. He had written an article or two on segregation in a book before he came here. He had no illusions about the fact that Negroes had not been given a fair shake. When I was on the legal subcommittee of the Governor's Advisory Committee on segregation in the public schools, I met with the Board of Directors of the Chamber of Commerce to try to get them to open businesses to whites and blacks alike. Their answer was, "We wouldn't touch it with a forty-foot pole." And when the sit-in strikes started and while Ed Burnside was Chairman of the Board of Directors of the Chamber of Commerce, they met and did recommend then to members and to businesses generally that they open their businesses, eating establishments or anything else to the public without regard to race. And that was done.

Marney was actually surprised and delighted at the action of the Chamber Board. I believe he came to my office and waited there while the Board of Directors was meeting.

—FRED HELMS

Archie Carroll felt that opening the restaurants in this manner

. . . was a bold step, a visionary step, and I can't see Ed Burnside doing that and disassociate that action and that approach from his relationship with Marney. Marney very specifically participated in this. I was Chairman of the Board of Deacons along about this time and a lot of the marchers who had been on the march in Selma, Alabama—the Selma-Montgomery march—came and had about a three day meeting. Marney invited them. A large number of people who had participated in that came and had a meeting right here in these rooms in this building, and I hadn't come quite as far along in my openness, maybe, at that time as I hope I am now, but I had come a long way for me. As chairman of the board I went to some of those sessions and heard some of those people speak and I was influenced to a greater awareness by being present with that group of people.

I think Marney changed us one by one—some of us. Some people got more rigid out of self-defense.

—Archie Carroll

I remember Marney talking about going to that meeting in which this restaurant integration was planned and coming out so very proud of the laymen, two of his own. He said he was weeping as he came out because of what he had seen his men do. This in a way was part of his contribution to the community. He did not do the visible things—like he was never president of the Ministers' Association or involved in a large way in the United Appeal. But he worked with this community of the church and the leadership in more intimate and personal ways. He was sort of in the background of what happened at the Chamber of Commerce. He didn't make speeches.

Marney gave a lot of support to a lot of people in the south that were struggling with these problems and there was a conference here. I remember one occasion that brought some of the wounded ones together. Ken Dean was here. He had been slashed with knives in Mississippi, and Clarence Jordan was here and a lot of people that were involved in the freedom rides and demonstrations. It was mainly an effort just to provide a presence. Just to say that Myers Park Church is open to this kind of person and that they were invited to be here for this meeting. I don't know how they came or who paid their way, but they were made to feel that there was an audience of support here. It was not a theological dialogue and it was not a meeting to plan any kind of change. Marney didn't operate that way. He was criticized for this by people who said he did not follow through in terms of programs or leadership or accepting a role as chairman of this or the other. But it wasn't his style. Presence was his style. I'm sure he carried on a correspondence with people who were involved in the struggle—the race struggle.

—CLAUDE BROACH

In his interview with oral historian Bill Finger in 1976, published later in CHRISTIAN CENTURY, Marney recalled,

I was a member of the committee at the Chamber of Commerce that opened the city on the black thing. The Chamber—that's where it was settled. I was amazed at the ethical awareness of some of the business leaders. But I read through their ethical language to see that what they were seeing was that, economically, this is a thing we had better do. But I didn't chide them for that. I was willing for it to happen for whatever reason.

What's the advantage of having 150,000 citizens buying grits and fatback instead of top-notch supplies? The difference is millions. What's the difference in having three branch banks on the right side of town or having 12 branch banks, six or eight of them black-operated? What's the point of having a really first-class black college if blacks can't get jobs?

The real issue in Charlotte never was race. It was economics, money, banking, interest rates, loan policies, employment. There's more economic determinism in capitalism than there ever was in communism, I think. So now all this crap we hear about profit being the soul of the nation simply means the nation's lost its soul to property.

During this era in Charlotte, Dr. Sam Byuarm, professor of sociology at Johnson C. Smith, discussed the issue with Marney.

I think during the 60's in this community Marney made a difference. I'm almost positive in some of the things they did he was constantly pressuring them or nudging them [members of his church] in the direction. He was constantly doing this directly or indirectly. For example, he may have made a statement out somewhere about what Myers Park Church needs to be doing, or what Myers Park Baptist can do.

Marney was a radical, the iron fist in the velvet glove. Radical as far as Myers Park Baptist was concerned. But there was sanity in what he was saying and what he was doing and they couldn't deny it. The sanity and the ethics—he had them on this.

I think that Marney in all probability felt that he had brought Myers Park Baptist Church as far as he was going to be able to carry it. That anything beyond that point would result in nothing but chaos to the future. They had done what they were going to do and

he wasn't satisfied with where they were, but in all probability it wasn't going any further. Time would have to pass. And, of course, this attitude that seemingly Marney attributed to Myers Park Baptist Church was in essence a microcosm of this community.

When it came to making changes in the area of racial issues, you didn't have an explosion in Charlotte. But the reason they didn't, we were always behind the scenes to some degree, pushing constantly. The community as such would dig in and they would sit right there until they saw the whites of their eyes again, and they moved back just enough to release the pressures, and you never got one of these explosions. I'm saying that Myers Park Baptist to me was a microcosm in Marney's mind of this kind of a thing. And it's hard on him. If you are the one who is the driving force, it takes a lot of energy.

Marney wasn't afraid, but he didn't want to become involved in an exercise in futility.

The Charlotte newspapers reported a few remarks Marney made in the community during the important period in the early sixties:

In 1961 Marney hired a Negro secretary, a Johnson C. Smith graduate, for his manuscript typing. "She's a good secretary. It did cause some concern, but from outside my church more than from within."

"Someone once asked me what I would do when a Negro presented himself for membership in our church. I will do two things. I will say, 'As of right now, I am this man's pastor.' Second, we will meet in two weeks to decide whether I am his pastor and your (the congregation) pastor, or just his pastor."

June 25, 1963, "My heart is bleak with the realization that there are 460 restaurants in Charlotte and about 460 churches, but one third of the restaurants are open (to both races). How many of our churches are open? The Church of Jesus Christ in Charlotte is not going to wait forever for the Chamber of Commerce, the restaurants, hotels and business people to wave our flags for us."

Marney told of meeting a parishioner on the street who complained of the lack of precedent for dealing with the Negro's current thrust for equality. "What precedent is there for the journey to Damascus?"

December 6, 1963, "It's been years since I asked the Lord to fix race relations in a town where he had a Baptist, Presbyterian, and Methodist majority."

February 28, 1964, "Have you hired any Negroes? Are you personally helping any family who's trying to climb out of poverty?

Do you have any friends whom you forget are white or non-white? Is there anybody across race lines you see just to see? If your answers aren't all yes, you aren't yet church."

May 25, 1964, preaching the baccalaureate sermon at Johnson C. Smith, "Some men can be trusted. May the years be good years to you and where they are not, may you have found enough men you can trust that bitterness becomes a kind of sweetness that offers some prospect for redemption for what you have endured."

In 1964 Johnson C. Smith University awarded two honorary doctorate degrees, one to Kays Gary of the Charlotte Observer for "distinguished service as a reporter and journalist," and to Carlyle Marney, "for his belief in the flexibility and malleability of human nature and his reminder, we are our brother's keeper"

Gary recalls,

It is true that Marney was extremely proud of this degree. At that time he was saying things and I was writing things that weren't popular, but were positive about the race issue. He caught a lot of flak and in some quarters was called too liberal.

And even after he left Myers Park, Marney wouldn't let the issue rest, an issue where race and relationship converged. Billy Pinson tells this story,

What I really remember about Marney is what he called "talk-backs" on Sunday nights. I listened. I never took any religion in college, but he was carrying on all this stuff, this "Theology", and I was coming from a Greenwood, S. C. background. Finally one day afterward I was talking to him and he said, "Well, Pinson, maybe you would do better if you found you another church." So right then I made up my mind that old SOB wasn't going to run me out of this church, so from then on I started taking a better look at what he was talking about. I just really bowed up and said he would never run me out of this church.

I think he was serious and needling me, too. Getting to me, because he knew how to work people. But I just kept arguing with him and told him I didn't agree with him. I took everything pretty literally in the Bible and never had really given it any deep thought until I came to this church; such things as the virgin birth and all that. You know, I just sort of took that at face value like it was told to me. He sort of changed my life then.

The other thing that really got to me with Marney was that we were over eating supper with friends one night when Marney was visiting and he got off on T. J. Reddy [of the Charlotte three]

when T. J. was in jail. He brought up the fact that T. J. had worked not at this church but through this church and he had been closely connected with him and he was a good man. He knew T. J. wasn't guilty of what he was charged with and that sentence was just awful. And he said it looked like some of the young men in this church ought to do something about it and get him out on bond. I was not thinking too much about it and started running my mouth and said I thought they should too. And three days later I got this letter from Marney explaining in detail what he would like for me to do. He wanted me to get some men in this church to put up the bond to get T. J. out of jail. So I started working on this and I worked and worked and could not get one living soul in this church to; nobody would touch it. And so I called Marney up and told him that we were running into great difficulty. It looked like there were just the two of us.

He said he still wanted to go through with it, so that left me with him and I went through it with him. My lawyer took the papers down to the lawyer and he said I was just an idiot to do this, but I said, "Well, I don't know really whether I'm right or wrong, but I'm going with Marney." He said, "Well, you will never see your money again." I thought you signed your name; I didn't know it was a cash bond, but I had to put cash money up and Marney did too. He said he was going to get his up some way and we put the bond up, not all of the bond, but it was part of it and I decided I had to take a stand. All these people talk about how religious they are and everything and how they want to do good, as long as it's really smooth. I could have gotten into some difficult situations because that was highly controversial at that time, but I felt like if it meant that much to him I would just donate my money if that's what it amounted to. I couldn't afford it. In fact, I had to borrow some of it. I didn't have the money because I didn't even know at the time things weren't too good with the stock market. This was when Marney had already left the church. But we got our money back. It really stuck with me, that he meant that much to me. I think I really was more concerned with backing Marney than backing T. J. Whether he was right or was wrong, I was going down swinging with him. I felt like he was right, but nobody else agreed with him. From a social standpoint, I understand why people don't want to do these things because the most of the people I come in contact with would be on the side of the judge. But one of the most conservative lawyers in this church, who would be right of William Howard Taft, said that he had to admit that whether he was guilty or not guilty that was a terrible sentence, unfair and unjust. My lawyer said he thought it was unfair too. He tried to get me to talk to the judge about it.

I might do it again. I guess I would have to say I believe in Marney that much to do it. Nobody else seemed to. They seemed to think he got off on these tangents. I think a group met and decided they wouldn't do anything about it. And I don't want you to think it was all that much money. It was like $2,500. We were just in it in a small way, but still it was big to us. It was something that I will never forget.

During the civil rights movement I remember one time he said he marched. Even though he was marching personally, he felt like we wanted him to march although we don't have many marchers at this church.

STIRRING THE POT

"I like to make people angry, because that's the way you find out who a person really is."

—CARLYLE MARNEY

Charlene Swansea grew up at Myers Park Baptist and recalls Marney warmly, but remembers,

We had a couple of interesting battles. One in particular. I was a charter member and demanded to get my church letter in my hands. Have you ever seen a church letter? No one has. They gave me a report card on my tithing. I was outraged.

I raised hell with Marney. Any place that would pass sterling silver collection plates and have a cosmetic gate that led nowhere, then give me a report card on tithing.

He said, "You're not going out of this church to no place. I know you better than that. Where are you going to go?"

I told him probably to the Friends' Meeting. From him came this deep sigh and he talked of his past history with the Quakers. I believe in his heart of hearts he was a pacifist, that Quakerism called to his inner convictions.

Fred Helms also recalls,

Marney and I had our differences in opinion. He became very much interested in this church being used as a halfway house for people who had nervous breakdowns and who had been in institutions for criminals. I was on the church committee that had this under consideration. As a member of the committee, I talked with John Rankin, then director of Memorial Hospital and formerly head of a large institution for nervous and mental and other patients. He was recognized as a national expert. I took the position that this was not the kind of location for a halfway house because it would have a religious connection that might be totally different from their own religion. There would be the danger to children and others by some of these people who were mentally unbalanced or criminals. Rankin said under no circumstances should a church undertake to be a halfway house. A halfway house should be unobtrusive and as confidential as possible. Marney and I took very different positions in the committee and, of course, he carried the committee. Then later I said, "Now you are wrong about this. . . ." But he abandoned the idea afterwards.

On another occasion in a deacons' meeting where payments of building fund pledges by members was under discussion, I said that

people who made their pledges and paid them were entitled to some commendation. That didn't appeal to Marney. He said, "Such pride is born of hell."

After the meeting I told Bill Schwantes, who had given the report, "You tell Marney tomorrow morning that he is as wrong as hell. The good works of anyone are subject to commendation and encouragement." Again I didn't say that in deacons' meeting. I said, "Tell Marney again it's more important that as leader of this church that he appear to be right, even when he is wrong."

Basically on most things I was in agreement with him—in his theology, philosophy and his preaching.

"To be able to disagree, yet to be able to understand and be reasonable is indeed a great trait; but Marney had it," recalls Hunter Jones.

I remember disagreeing with him once in particular. At some meeting in the early days of integration, he made a statement that he had been talking to one or two of the Negro leaders in Charlotte. He perhaps named them, but off-hand I can't remember. He hoped that one or two of them would see fit to join our church. As soon as the meeting was over and he started to walk out, young Dr. Charles Jarrett and myself stopped him and we were a little concerned that his feeling would be to go out and invite someone of the opposite race to join our church. We told him that if anyone of the opposite race in true sincerity wanted to join, to walk down the aisle and present himself for membership in our church, we certainly would not oppose it and would vote for it. But, we could not see going out and soliciting just to be able to tell the rest of Charlotte or whomever that we have them as members. He frowned and said, "you all would want to keep us, or me, from having some integration in the church?" and we said, "No not at all; but we would not want to have it done by solicitation. We would want it done by the same invitation that all members of this church have. That they are invited to walk down the aisle if they want to join and we feel that should be the same way and not otherwise." And he in his usual good grace said, "Well, that's certainly all right." That's the only real confrontation I ever had with him.

He said at the time, "If you don't really go out and make it a personal effort to get someone to cross a line, they aren't." I think Marney may have invited some of his contacts. . . . "Why don't you join us?" But I don't think he ever did try to do it by direct invitation and have everybody join in that. If he did, I never knew anything about it. It was never discussed again as far as I know.

—HUNTER JONES

He and my father used to get into some terrible arguments about economics. There were some good businessmen here. They didn't mind telling him real quick about what they thought about the world of business and economics. Marney never claimed to be an expert in the field of economics, "I'm an advocate of the free enterprise system without fully understanding it."

—STUART DICKSON

He was an infuriating man to work with. I had to adopt the ground rule early that he would win. I would argue, then as soon as I stopped he'd switch sides and give evidence to support my side.

—CAREY DOWD

When Sarah Bryant was President of the Women of the Church, she remembers:

Marney brought me into focus. There was something going on that I wanted to have happen and I was very disappointed because it didn't come off. I cried over it, I was so frustrated. He said, "Sarah, do you really ever think that there would be a corporate action on anything by the congregation? Do you think it's realistic to believe that?" I was thinking there could be something everybody would agree to do, that you could finally bring everybody together. . . .Well, he brought me into focus by saying it isn't realistic to believe you are going to get everybody going in the same direction.

Marney was not everybody's man. And people who are afraid to get at the nitty gritty by themselves couldn't take that. They got angry with him.

—CLAUDE BROACH

Marney and I had great arguments about immortality. . . . I remember walking down the steps with him one time. The lesson had been on life after death. I said, "Marney, I just can't go along with what you said. How can you be sure?" He said, "Well, I'm not sure, but you can hope."

—PRISCILLA UPCHURCH

Possibly one of the longest running of Marney's confrontations was with the Southern Baptist Convention:

He was very critical of the Southern Baptist Convention. He had no sympathy at all with the politics of it. Twenty-five years ago and more, Baptists used to look down on the Roman Catholic Church and call it political ecclesiasticism because of their political influence worldwide. And now we have come to realize that is what the Southern Baptist Convention is. And Marney saw that. He thought that that had no relationship to the Kingdom of God. The politics of it just turned him off.

I don't expect he thought he could change it. If he wanted to change it, he would have become a part of it and worked from within. But, he didn't have that kind of patience. If he had gone to the Baptist Pastors' conferences and the Baptist denominational meetings, I think he could have had a tremendous influence and maybe spared us some of the troubles that we have had, some of the divisiveness that's come about locally. But, Marney didn't have that kind of patience. It would have been boring for him to sit there. Torture really. But if he had done it, with his personality, he might have made some changes because the people who have a bad image of Marney never really knew Marney. He was the most winsome person. I think he could have won any of them almost. They might not have agreed with him, but they would have loved him.

—Ed Echerd

Ed Echerd's optimism is generous in the light of statements by Marney which appeared in the local papers in 1964:

A social revolution is going on, but we Baptists who are on God's right hand had precious little to do with it except when run over from the rear.

* * * * * *

When Baptists come to a fork in the road, you don't fork at all. You go right on!

* * * * * *

The American Baptist Convention would be swallowed like a ticking hand grenade by the larger Southern Baptist Convention and who could live long with a live hand grenade in his stomach?

* * * * * *

There are hundreds of colleges and dozens of seminaries and scores of Baptist organizations which provide little kingdoms which little men just love to run. They won't give up their thrones for unity's sake.

* * * * * *

The Southern Baptist Convention is a Jesus cult dressed like Buster Brown and Little Lord Fauntleroy with a bowie knife handy to cut the throats of any who disagree with a regional point of view.

* * * * * *

And if it appears Marney went easy on the American Baptist Convention, he didn't.

The ABC is in danger of being consumed by its own smugness.

Provocative adversary, potent prophet, a worrisome horsefly buzzing the grazing herd, Marney liked to fight, so much so that he even fought when he didn't have to. He sparred for fun.

LET THE CHILDREN COME

Marney may have been a high-class but earthy intellectual as well as an awesome personage capable of biting sarcasm, but he was also clay in the hands of children. He didn't hide it. Some of his best sermon stories embellished the perceptive remarks of neighborhood children along with the heady names of the other theologians he so often quoted.

For several church families Marney's vulnerability to children made all the difference.

Helen Goans remembers:

The night my husband Jack died so suddenly with a heart attack, Bud Wilmot came to our house. The boys, ages 5, 8, 11, and almost 12, were asleep. Bud was in great distress because he could not get Marney and he knew he was in town. A tree had fallen on his telephone line and the phone was out and nobody knew it. We did not see him until the next morning some time.

He spent a lot of special time with the boys. These were the kinds of things he did: Our first Saturday night alone he and Elizabeth had been somewhere and they came by the house. I'll never forget it. A friend had brought the holes of doughnuts she had made and they were very tempting to Marney. He should not have eaten them. We assured him that since they were holes, they had no calories and he just kept eating. He visited in the bedroom with the boys and talked with them.

It just seemed like any night my doorbell would ring and it would be Marney. He would be on his way somewhere and he would come in and tuck Jim in bed and kiss him goodnight and talk to the big boys. It was almost like 'When you need me, I'll be around. You don't even know you need me now, but the boys do.' He came when I didn't even know we needed him. He would spend time with each one briefly, walk back to their bedrooms and would be on his way.

The other thing I remember his doing shortly after Jack died. When he left after one of their alone times, the boys came out wide-eyed and said, 'Do you know what Marney taught us? He taught us his phone number and we can call him anytime we need him and he will always be there. We know his office number and his home number.' That was like security in their pockets. I don't know if they ever used it, but they knew they could.

. . . Marney knew that I had worked at the airlines. There were times I needed to talk with him about some direction. One morning I stopped by the office about a month or so after Jack died, and I

told him I came to get clearance from the tower. He said, 'I can't give you clearance, but I can give you a weather report.' We talked about the decisions I had made about where we would live and how we would operate. Bud had asked me if I would teach over here at the church and Marney said, 'Well, you are, aren't you?' I told him I felt like Bud had created that job to meet my needs. He said it amazed everybody how Bud could reach down in his drawer and find an available person if he needed somebody. From time to time he would just check in and see how we were and what we had been doing.

I could be a good Presbyterian. I think sometimes things were predestined. . . . I always felt that someone better than me planned for Marney to be here.

Helen Goans kept the letters Marney wrote her family. The following are excerpts:

December 22, 1966 Waynesville

. . . I am here with a sleepy dog, beautiful snow, bright sun, lazy fire and a long list of letters to answer. Tell all the boys at your house that I miss them just about the most of all. I am exercising more now. It cuts the post-op pain. Cut wood for an hour this morning—felt good to swing something!

All my love to all of you.

MARNEY
(Handwritten)

Dear Jim Goans - I'LL BET YOU CAN READ PRINT BETTER THAN CURSIVE WRITING. (That's this kind) SO I WILL TRY TO PRINT. BUT ITS HARD!

THANK YOU FOR YOUR CARD AND NOTE. I HOPE YOU AND ALL YOURS ARE WELL. AND I HOPE YOU LIKE BEING SEVEN YEARS OLD.

ITS COLD. I'VE BEEN SPLITTING WOOD. WILL SEE YOU SOON.

LOVE
MARNEY

April 14, 1967 Lake Junaluska

All I know is you'll just have to make an excursion up here with all four of your men—so we can all see how the land lies (on its side) and how E. and I are doing. I don't want to get too scattered.

Tell your youngest Indian that I'm having bear trouble and need all of them to help me run off these big bad black bears from my orchard! When can you come up for a day?

Love,
MARNEY

May 26, 1967 Interpreters' House

Dear Helen and Boys:

Your letter tells me again how fortunate I have been these years and especially since September—in my friends. Some have had to be long-suffering with me for at times I am weeks behind.

Our little red house (2 rooms, a kitchen and bath), a red barn (3 stalls), and a rock apple house forty feet square for a living room-office continues to be the best place on earth for us to live. My office at Lambuth Inn is a far cry from that nice mahogany and walnut job I was flying at Charlotte—But we are underweight! Interpreters' House has been chartered, a board being named, first materials created and printed, and our staff is planned and contracted. I am putting you on our list to get all mailings—more later.

Meanwhile know of our continuing concern and regard for you and yours—and don't pass through here without stopping.

Let me hear when you can come up.

Yours,
MARNEY

May 10, 1971 Interpreters' House

Our dear Helen and her men: [after their grandfather's death]

There's a time for death. When it is on time, as with my father at 83, one can celebrate.

When it is premature and off schedule—we grieve the more and more.

You and all yours have exceeded all my hopes in your great victory—never—complete.

Love,
MARNEY

Connie and Bob Maccubbin were another church family who came to know Marney through their children. Connie recalls,

I never even knew Marney except to hear him in the pulpit. I was in awe of him until we had a little boy who became ill with leukemia. The first time he came to see me at the hospital I had been

having a lot of people come to see me praying and trying to say everything is going to be all right. He came and he cried and said, "How can you go through this?" And he told me of the experience he had with his daughter Susan, who when she was younger had almost died . . . the pain, the grief, and the hurt! It was my first experience with a minister not trying to say that God is going to make everything all right, but just hurting with you.

Danny was 21 months old and loved Dr. Marney. In the hospital Marney took Danny for a ride in the wheelchair. They just took to each other. When we came home, Marney came to see us and he would get down on the floor with our other little boy who was four years old. The three of them would roughhouse. Marney just popped in, never called to say he was coming. One time he brought that Jeep Waggoneer out and took them all to ride. Really special and warm. Danny called him Marney Maccubbin. That really got to him. He said Danny let him in.

When Danny died, Marney wasn't in town, but he had been so special to us that we waited a few days more than the normal time so he could do the funeral. He said just the right things, used the scripture about David and his son dying. We had said, "Don't make it sentimental, because we don't think we will be able to stand it." He said the things that made it complete.

I didn't see him much afterwards. He called me and I guess I was afraid to get too close to him. He would ask how I was doing and I would say, "Fine." He tried to follow through. Later I wrote him a letter telling him how much he had meant to us and he wrote me back. I guess he kind of kept me in reality, because I had become very involved with people who believed in faith healing and, you know, anything can happen if you pray and if you believe. So he kept me in balance realizing that things aren't always all right. That was one of the things that helped me when Danny died, to be able to accept. I always felt, that God doesn't choose. We have diseases and we die young. I just don't believe in a God like that.

One thing that he said to my mother really stuck with me. We were sitting out in the back yard and my mother was apologizing that she never went to church. He said, "I think you have church right here." And that took some guilt away. She doesn't feel she needs to apologize anymore.

He was probably the least churchy man I've ever met. He acted and looked like someone who really didn't care what people thought about him and was not trying to be anybody's deliverer. He really let you know he was being delivered too.

One of our sons was hit by a car. I don't know how he heard about it, but Marney got to the hospital soon after the ambulance and stayed and stayed and stayed. Now he was a busy man, but that pastoral presence seemed to be there when the time called for it. Lots of people expected him to come if they had a bad cold, but when you had real troubles and real needs and I remember other members of the family who were ill, he was present—just showed up and it wasn't that he dropped in and said hello and said a word of prayer, but he stayed, very relaxed, smoking that pipe, very quiet, would keep the conversation going and just somehow found the things to say or sit close to you and say nothing.

T. J. NORMAN

And Nancy Geer tells this story.

I remember best his love of children, mine and other people's. Any time I came to the church with my children he would invite us all into his office. The children would be the focus of his attention. One of the first encounters my children had with him, he took them into his office and talked to them for a few minutes. Then he said, "Look around and whatever you see that you want, you can have." I thought, 'Oh, my goodness,' for his office was filled with what it looked to me were priceless things that he would not want to part with—treasures—and the children would pick things invariably that were perfectly all right with him. But I think if they had chosen his most prized object, he would have given it to them. He put no restrictions on what they could have. One day John chose (and still has) a pen set some club in Austin had given Marney. On it was a little flag of Texas. He gave that to John and I can't remember what Susie chose. Susie was three and John was seven or eight. Generally, when I had the children, I was just over here at the church and had not come to see him specifically. I did see Marney often at one point because I was having some problems with nightmares. I didn't know what was happening. I was afraid I was on the verge of something, maybe a breakdown. I couldn't sleep. So I came over to talk to him about that and I still feel a great deal of gratitude to him because he helped me to focus on something in my life that I had suppressed for years. It was causing my nightmares. He was the best head shrinker in town at that time, and his price was very reasonable.

Maybe his fatherliness made him approachable at the time. When I first met Marney I was a very vulnerable, insecure person. My need for his wisdom and guidance superceded any fear that I might have had. I sensed a warmth and a depth and competence that he had and I needed. There was a lot of trust there for me. That continued and he never did anything to allay that. I still have that feeling for Marney, even though I have lost my need for an authority figure. I have had a little guilt about that, because I feel that he really was the kind of person that we kind of picked to pieces, and maybe denied him his personhood. We set him up on a pedestal and expected all sorts of things of him. I am not very sure that there was much reciprocity there. I wish there had been, in retrospect, because I think that may be the reason he had to leave the church. We didn't give him enough of what he needed, for him to be able to stay.

When I went to him one time, I told him I didn't know what my problems were stemming from. I told him I was afraid they were personal and that I was a very immature person. He listened to me talk and at the end of the first session I had with him he said, "Nancy, your problem is not immaturity," and I said, "How do you know? You don't know me well enough to say." And he said, "I can tell more from a person's use of personal pronouns than anything they say." I thought that was very interesting and I try to focus on that sometimes when I talk with somebody, to hear how much they are I and me and when they focus on others.

He made such a difference in my life—mainly the nightmare situation. I feel Marney just took my life and gave it back to me. I really thought I had lost it. When I was just ten months old, my father locked me in a room and threatened to kill me and himself. My mother couldn't get to me. I had never heard this story from my mother. I had only heard it from my grandmother and an aunt. My mother remarried when I was ten. For those first ten years of my life I had no sense of history because I did not know my father. I had this tremendous sense of unknowing of something so bad that it couldn't be talked about. It came out in nightmares.

I didn't know what was happening in the nightmares. I just knew that I was waking up with this seven foot tall figure standing over me. I would reach out and scream and reach for him and he would not be there. I would literally have tears on my face it would be so real. At that point I was afraid to go to sleep and was having insomnia. My children were little and I guess they were my saving grace. When I told Marney about this, I went to him not having any idea why I was having this nightmare and he started asking me questions about my childhood and I told him this story. I didn't even know if it is true or not; that I had never heard the story from my mother. He said, "Nancy, it isn't important if it is true. It is important that it is in your head. What gives credence to the truth is that the figure is so large. To babies, adults are giants." I told him I couldn't remember that far back. And he said you can remember all the way back to the womb.

HE WHO HAS EARS TO HEAR, LET HIM HEAR

The quality of listening attention and help Marney gave Nancy Geer was not an unusual incident. Repeatedly in the interviews persons recalled and described the unique way Marney called them out, listened and was present to them.

Dr. Sam Byuarm recalls,

This had always been an abiding interest of his, this business of counselling. He made this observation I have never forgotten. He says to me, "Sam, you know when you are the pastor of a church and you are dealing with people and they come to you for advice; when they come seeking information of various sorts, always keep in mind that 99 times out of 100 that person is actually seeking answers to questions he has not asked." Marney's argument was that you had to be attuned to this. . . . Until you accept that fact, you are not going to be much of a counselor.

Harriett Fortenberry came to see Marney. She remembers,

The first real conversation I had with Marney (I was twenty-five), he kept saying to me, "I just don't understand what makes you bubble." So we had this conversation and God only knows how long I talked before I stopped, probably half an hour. I'll never forget how he leaned back in his chair and started tapping his fingers like this, rocking back and forth and he said, "I hear the words you use. I hear the words you don't use. I hear the words you load."

"Load?"

"Yeah, I heard the words you load." And then in essence it happened that Marney had called my bluff. And he was for me, my first listener. He was the first person other than my husband who listened and took me seriously. So what his response did to me at the time upset me deeply and I remember driving home and I had to pick up a child way far from home. I remember driving and thinking, "I don't care. I don't care what he thinks of me. What would I care? Who is he? What do I care?" And I really interpreted his not buying my act with a disregard or devaluing of me.

I wrote him a letter, let me tell you, and I got this note back that said, "How strange that you should have felt that way, because I was thinking how worth knowing you are." This assuaged the violent feelings of rejection that I had. Subsequently we never really talked again. I don't have a long standing, shared relationship with Marney. Marney left me alone. Coming from Roman Catholicism I was not jumping into Myers Park Baptist Church. I remember asking him, "Why do people keep telling me believe, and you will be saved? I don't understand what that means." And he would just say, "They just don't know what else to say." Somehow he was a comrade in my uncertainty, which I do believe he was always.

When I joined the church, he had been gone for awhile. I was driving down the street and saw him at the church. I rolled the window down and just screamed because I had to get the message across the street to the church door where he was standing with all these people. "Hey, Marney, I joined the church!" Everybody turned. You would have thought I'd been to some revival and was still caught up in the whole thing. They all stared very indignantly and Marney just nodded and said, "Good. Good," and I drove off.

There was no need to do a whole lot about whatever we shared. But when Marney had a very rough time I thought, "Well, damn, when there's sadness in a time of a life you care about, you want to be with them." And I thought I don't know him well enough to even say, "Hey, you're not on top of the mountain anymore either and I know it." At the time I was storytelling and one of the stories the children really loved was about Gloomy Erasmus. Gloomy Erasmus was a great big bear and he was so gloomy because nobody really loved him that much or liked him. They didn't play with him much in the forest and he didn't have any function, there was nothing he really did, and it was just a pretty bad time for him until somebody discovered that on hot summer days he cast a very nice long cool shadow. I realized that this is what Marney did for Myers Park. He cast a long cool shadow and he was so big himself that there were so few who could do the same for him. So I wrote him about Gloomy Erasmus.

There was no way Marney didn't have frailties. They were hanging out all over him. I never got the feeling he made all that much effort to hide them, they seemed so obvious. It was sort of part and parcel. They all go together and I'm not going to get ecstatic over the great part and I'm not going to be brutal with negatives, whatever they are.

With young Stuart Dickson, Marney's approach was novel and nervy: *Marney was never short on nerve. I remember very distinctly that I was then in the investment banking business and Marney had been here, I guess, two or three years. Long enough that we knew each other, but not all that well. The phone rang one day and he said, "Stuart, this is your preacher."*

I said, "Hello, Dr. Marney. What can I do for you?"

"Well," he said, "I want to spend a little bit of time with you on something. Where do you eat lunch?"

I said, "Oh, I eat all around."

He said, "Don't you eat lunch at the City Club most every day?"

I said, "No, I get over there occasionally."

He said, "Well, I enjoy going. How about us meeting over there for lunch? What are you doing tomorrow?"

I told him nothing that couldn't be moved around. So we made a date. I had no idea what he was interested in or after. Met him over at the City Club at twelve noon. We went in and sat down and he said, "Do you have a drink at lunch?"

I said, "No, sir, not ordinarily."

"Well," he said, "I just want you to maybe sort of show me what you did downtown. Let's have one."

I said, "Well, you're the preacher in town. If it doesn't bother you, it's not going to bother me." So we ordered a cocktail, believe it or not, and sat down to lunch and he said, "Tell me what you are doing."

I said, "I'll be glad to."

I put in a lunch order and talked about what my job was, what I was doing. He would interrupt me a few times with a question about this or that. I realized at the end of about forty minutes I had been talking all about myself and what I was doing and what the company I was with was doing, what we were involved in and we'd just about finished lunch and I hadn't learned a thing about what Marney wanted. With that realization I sort of stopped. He said, "Well, go on."

I said, "Well, I don't know anything else to say. I have told you what I am doing."

"Well," he says, "it sounds to me like you've got your life all figured out. You've got a nice pasture you're living in with a fence around it. Sounds to me like there are a few other horses in the pasture that you are grazing with and enjoying living with. And I would offer the observation that you've got it all figured out and just down pat, and haven't got the faintest idea what's on the other side of the fence."

Well, I was put down real quick. And then he went on and said, "Let me tell you about some of the things we are doing and thinking about wanting to do and I would like to get you involved in." It turned out I set my own trap and in effect opened it wide for Marney.

It was what he didn't say that made you stop and think. At that lunch he paraphrased in about three minutes what I had spent forty-five minutes telling him with all the enthusiasm and excitement that I could muster as a young fellow about what I was doing and why I was doing it. His was about as good a put-down as you could have in the way—"That's wonderful. A nice fence around a perfectly laid plan for your own comfort and enjoyment. Let me tell you what some other people are doing."

I think what he said did make a difference. I don't think, I know it did. I guess it was the first time I had ever given any thought or considered that there was an obligation, real obligation, a community obligation, that feeling of you've got to put more in than just your career, just your family, just your own personal comfort. I would date any real look-see at outside my own paddock, so-to-speak, at the words he laid out at that particular time. I had been involved in some other things other than my own business, but I'd never understood that involvement was almost a "somebody asked you, so you had to do it, sort of an I.O.U. basis." He opened up a spectre of the why. What was out there? What could be, how big and how enormous it was to try at least to put something in. Just a unique way of doing it. I think any other way you would have resented it. Or I would have. Or I would have said, "Here is another preacher trying to preach to me about what I should do." That wasn't his approach at all. It was just "Let's have lunch. Tell me what you are doing." He let me talk myself right into how wrong I was without any problem at all.

* * * * * *

Marney could remember all sorts of things. Could quote verbatim what you said. Then I became concerned that I'd better be careful, but he never violated that. He'd quote you, but always in context.

—T. J. NORMAN

Claude Broach recalls,

We were never together for long stretches of time, but we were together in a lot of conversations. I remember a conversation that extended over quite a lengthy period. That was a time when I was trying to decide whether to accept an invitation to leave Charlotte and teach at Southern Seminary in Louisville. A few people were aware of what was going on and the decision I was wrestling with. Marney was one of them. I think he had a good bit to do with my decision not to go. Not that he told me not to go, but in sorting things out and deciding where I wanted to be and what kind of person I wanted to be in terms of vocation and career and life style and so on. He was very helpful, because I think he knew my strengths and weaknesses. Since he had been involved in teaching much more recently than I had, he helped me see some of the things that I think I would have overlooked in terms of making a decision like that. He had a very real gift for helping somebody to discover something on his own. He didn't tell you this about yourself or give advice in this way, but by asking probing questions or by pushing you on into something you were about to say yourself, he would develop some insights about your own mind that came out in indirect ways, but very different, positive ways. It was a great talent.

—CLAUDE BROACH

Back in '63 or thereabouts I had in my family situation some problems that were pretty serious and fanned out to affect some of my business relationships. I was hurting pretty bad and leaned on Marney. I got to Marney and he was hard to get to sometimes, all of his studies and everything else, but he was pretty open to me. I went to visit him in his library on Providence Road where he was living then. I've been to his house at six o'clock in the morning once or twice to get to see him. He'd been up by four o'clock anyway. Marney's toughness, roughness, bluntness and yet his terrific sensitivity to seeing the truth, his downright help with problems are qualities I remember. He strongly influenced my life.

—ARCHIE CARROLL

YARNING

People soon learned that although Marney respected personal confidences in a thoroughly professional manner, he was not to be trusted with a humorous story. He was a truly talented thief.

Bob Bryant remembers,

When I was at Green Lake, Wisconsin, the American Baptist Assembly Grounds, I was playing golf with a man I met there. When he discovered I was from Marney's church, he began to tell me a story Marney had told him, a wonderful story about Marney's aunt. She kept a thundermug (chamberpot) under her bed at night.

One night Marney and some of the others put alka-seltzer into the jar and waited downstairs to see what would happen. They waited and waited until later, when the warm liquid hit the alka-seltzer, they heard their aunt cry out, "Children, children come quick! Something's bad wrong!"

It's a great story, but it wasn't Marney's aunt at all. It happened to my aunt and I had told the story to Marney. I couldn't wait to get back to Charlotte and get him with that one.

Marney also exaggerated stories about his organist in Austin. Paul Kennard, the organist, made the mistake of telling Marney his experience of sitting very near a famous concert pianist who performed in a large hall. The organist overheard the performer say to himself at the end of a mighty flourish on the keyboard, "God, wasn't that beautiful!"

Marney loved the story; only his version, which he repeated all over the southwest, was about the organist himself practicing arpeggios in his empty sanctuary exclaiming, "God, wasn't that beautiful!"

That same organist had the misfortune of forgetting the open baptistry one Monday morning. He intended to go into the door to the organ chamber, but fell into the filled baptistry instead. And Marney added that story also, embellished, of course, to his own repertoire.

Another example of a Marney-ized story is cited by Nancy Geer,

When our daughter Susie was four years old, she had a serious illness and was in the hospital for four or five days. . . . I remember Marney's coming up to the hospital to see her on several different occasions while she was there. Once I had gone home when Marney came to see Susie. When I got back to the hospital a Nun came up to me and said, "Your minister came to see Susie while you were gone. We were teasing Susie about him and asked her if she knew who that man was. She said, 'Yes, he is our creature.' "

I told Marney about this at the time it happened and we had a big laugh about it. In a videotaped interview with Marney in 1978 about his feeling about the church, Marney told this story. But, it wasn't about Susie. He said it was about this young lady at Duke University. Well, bless his heart, he was human like the rest of us. He got his stories mixed up. Either that or it could have happened twice. He possibly made it into a better story. That's closer to the truth.

Marney's version of the story was,

I remember flapping along to the Great Hall in my robe. I hadn't even changed from the sanctuary, hearing a lovely little three year old from behind say to her momma, "There goes our creature."

I saw her recently at Duke University where she's a junior.

* * * * * *

Jim Berry remembers,

Marney told a good one on me. Jim Middleton at the First Baptist Church in Shreveport was trying to get me to leave Austin and come to Shreveport. It was a larger church. He talked to me on the phone about it for about 45 minutes and I told him I wasn't particularly interested in leaving. He kept on calling so I decided to go over and see him. Marney knew all about it because Jim was a good friend of his and Jim told him what he was doing. Finally I told Marney, "I have told him over and over that I'm not interested." Marney said, "If you've really made up your mind, then I'll stop it." He called Jim and said, "Jim, I wish you'd leave Berry alone. He hasn't been here very long, but he's been here just about long enough. You know, he's an alcoholic and we've just about got him over the hill." So I never heard anymore from Jim Middleton.

Berry continues,

Marney always laughed about the time, not too long after being in Austin, when I was trying to get the music level higher. He went to Baylor University for a meeting and somebody asked him if they could bring what he thought was the Baylor Choir to the church in Austin. "Why, of course." He accepted without saying anything to me about it. It turned out to be the Baptist Student Union Choir and that was a lot different. They came down with their blue lights and their glittering letters that they strung out across the front of the church and they did the most gosh awful kind of music that I have ever been exposed to. Marney claimed I never forgave him for that.

I don't remember that there was anything so terrible about it, but he could also make a good story out of anything.

Haynes Baird has further evidence,

Marney had this habit of taking a story and changing it. I've been accused of the same thing. Anyway, he told this one on me. He said that I was out digging in my yard one day and this lady came along riding in a Cadillac with a chauffeur and she stopped and looked at me and said, "Hey, boy, you're doing a right good job there. How much would you charge to work for me?" And Marney said I looked at the lady and said. "Well, this lady here lets me sleep with her." And then Marney added how she took off in a huff and so on.

That never happened to me at all. One little thread of truth is that I have done a little yard work. Emily Heaton asked me once, "Who in the world planted your landscape?" I told her I did. And she said, "I thought so."

THE CHARLOTTE NEWS

A COMPANY OF BROTHERS

"A man can relate to men. He can become all men. He can be redeemer. And in this redemption of relation he can live."

Marney, The Recovery of the Person

Marney could communicate—children, women, men, illiterates, theologians, animals. He could connect with anyone and he did. But most remarkable for his time and place, white upper middle class south in the 50's and 60's, were his many strong and deep relationships with men.

Perhaps it was his rough exterior, his old clothes and commanding presence, profanity, hard drinking, hard driving, the whole Texas-Tennessee mythic context of mountain, horse, ranch, and pasture. Or more possibly the real key may have been simply his colorful directness, his sensitive intelligence, and his rare humor.

Marney made the address to the annual meeting of the Charlotte YMCA one year. He started his remarks,

Always a pleasure to be in front of a group of people or an organization like the YMCA particularly at a meal. I could certainly tell that I am in the midst of such an organization from the smell emanating from the walls and floors.

—Stuart Dickson

Jim Berry recalls Marney's speaking to a Boy Scout Leaders' Conference in Houston, Texas to 300-500 men.

He got up for his speech telling jokes and carrying on. So help me, I have never heard so many men laugh so hard and so long. From where I was sitting I could see one man down on the floor beating the floor, he was laughing so hard. Then Marney would turn it around and really put the screws to what he was saying. When he got through, they stood and applauded for five minutes.

Lex Marsh remembers,

I persuaded him to join the YMCA Health Club. All the masseuers are blind. They are great conversationalists and always kid each other. The first time I took Dr. Marney down he was accepted by them right quick. A month or two later I went up to the health club and one of the masseuers said, "Dr. Marney, can you save my soul?" and Marney said, "Oh, yes I think I can, but I don't know if it would be worth the trouble."

He came out to the house to ride horseback when he was in

town. I found out he not only liked to ride but he liked to groom the horses, to feed them. He just liked the atmosphere of a barn. It was relaxation for him to come out and feed his horses. We had an agreement that any time he couldn't come to feed them that I would take care of it and we sort of alternated. But, even though I was supposed to feed on certain days, half the time he would be out there. He was maybe running away from stress of the hard studying he was doing, into a brand new atmosphere. We had some very enjoyable moments.

I looked forward to my first trip with him. He decided we would take the horses up to Waynesville, North Carolina. His good friend, Dr. Jim Fowler, invited us to come up and bring our horses and have three or four days with him. We borrowed a truck and loaded our horses early one morning and Marney drove the truck. I learned some little things about him, one of which is that he drank more coffee than anybody I ever did see, so he fixed up two thermos bottles of hot coffee. So we had to stop about once every hour and drink coffee. We stopped for a red light at a main crossing and Marney's jug of hot coffee fell out of the truck. The thermos rolled down the hill under a gate of a big industrial plant and we had a minor crisis in retrieving that coffee. We finally persuaded a guard to hand it to us and we continued the trip.

The first night he brought a book along and we had a very pleasant visit with this host of ours, who put us both up in the same bedroom with two beds. I was ready to go to sleep by ten or ten-thirty, but Marney read that book almost all night. I know I waked up about one and he was still reading the book and I persuaded him to go to sleep. He waked up again about five o'clock and started reading again, so I told him the next day, "You know, I was in bed eight hours and I only got three hours of sleep on account of you." And he said, "Well, that is all you needed."

Edna Alsdurf, Marney's secretary at Myers Park and later at Interpreters' House, watched a remarkable parade as she worked at the door of Marney's Charlotte office.

Hardly a week went by that somebody from somewhere out of town didn't come by to see him. In fact, they came in droves from all over the country, young seminary men, older ministers, men who heard him speak off somewhere, knew he was somebody they could talk to. If they could get here to this part of the country, they'd come by.

Marney had wide-ranging friendships in far-flung places to an extraordinary degree (which is another story in itself); but by the way he interacted with the persons at Myers Park, the men in particular, on horseback trips, around campfires, study groups, counselling, arguing over issues and then through the throes of his heart attack and departure, certainly these persons and Marney, as they experienced the dense terrain of relationship, knew they were becoming Church.

Marney told Sarah Bryant, "You know, as hard as it is and as much as I think sometimes it doesn't come off, I've never known more church than I've known here."

He told Fred Helms, "This is the damnedest church I've ever seen anywhere and this is the church I want to remain a member of as long as I live."

CARRIED OUT

The Charlotte Observer reported on September 5, 1966:

Dr. Carlyle Marney, Charlotte's nationally known Baptist Minister, became ill between services and was taken by ambulance to Memorial Hospital. The fifty year old pastor . . . had been talking with William Schwantes, church administrator, about details for an afternoon funeral. Earlier he had preached the 8:30 service, taught Sunday School lesson, and had returned to Charlotte a week ago from a six-week lecture tour ranging from Florida to upstate New York.

While he was in the hospital, news came from Washington in late September that President Lyndon Johnson had appointed him to a special national advisory commission on the problems of rural poverty.

And from the Charlotte News, October 11, 1966:

Dr. Marney is to be released from the hospital October 12. He is recovering from "heart damage" and will be under doctors' close supervision when he leaves the hospital for his mountain cabin near Waynesville. He will remain in the mountains for continued recuperation.

Priscilla Upchurch talks about Marney's life with Myers Park:

I heard him say he felt in the membership of 1600 he had no more than 300, and that was an outside figure. Those 300 were a unit that would go along—that he was influencing and had influenced. . . .

I think Marney just worked himself to death . . . burned the candle at both ends. He smoked too much, and wouldn't sleep. He would get up at 2 A. M. and study. His habit was not to sleep an ordinary night's sleep . . . if he had lived longer he had so much more to give and everybody said he did two people's work in his lifetime. And they say that if he had lived longer he could have done three people's work.

T. J. Norman:

I think Marney became a poet while he was here, a person in need of the congregation that surrounded him. He could be terribly blustery, make caustic remarks, but I think in later years here, he evidenced a great deal of affection and need for his people surrounding him. He responded to their need, but he needed them too. It was a mutual putting arms around each other.

He went as a different Marney to the mountains. At first he wouldn't let people get close to him. As time moved on, that barrier seemed to dissolve and after a major illness developed, he reached a point of wanting his friends around him. I didn't notice this fortress-like person there.

Good Friday, 1967
Wolf Pen Mountain

The Congregation and
The Board of Deacons
Myers Park Baptist Church
Charlotte, North Carolina

Beloved Community:

It is time today to give answer to the gracious letter the Deacons sent last September. I have carried it seven months, with its assurances and its gracious insistence that all the time I should need was mine. I am profoundly grateful for it, as for the hundreds of more private expressions that have come. Now I see my way, and to take more of your generosity would be hurtful for you and prolong the strain of uncertainty on me.

First, I must say this: My situation is in no way an effect of the pastorate of Myers Park Baptist Church. No people ever made less demand; none were ever easier to serve; no staff was ever better formed, and work was never better divided. Nor is there anywhere a more precious and effective local community. I found Church with you and all my ways and days will bear the mark of what you gave me, taught me, suffered me to learn among you.

Circumstances utterly beyond my control or desire turn me from you. I have literally preached myself into the contradiction which now requires my resignation, or I become denier of the light and a castaway. You have heard me vow to follow any new light I could get; you have known me to be a candidate for any post that would put me nearer the center of the sea of troubles that now beset the Great Church; and, you heard me find my way to the Interpreters' House. This is where I must abide for now. I shall be trying to live among the clergy and laity of a vast region in an Interpreters' House at Lambuth Inn, Lake Junaluska, just what I have learned from the Interpreters' House I found at Myers Park Baptist Church. Such a joy as we have had must be one that will share well.

Did ever a man preach himself out of a dearer, lovelier place? I would have stayed with you, and fattened on your generosity forever, except for last September. And now you must do two things; you must be Church, and you must gladly let me go. I have done all I know to you. My resignation should take effect at once, though I confess that every day, Sundays especially, and every Holy Week in particular, I shall long for Camelot and wish I were back. So will Elizabeth to whom you are dear.

I did not come willingly to your high pulpit—and as all of you know, I did not come down willingly or willfully. You might say I was carried in, and carried out. But the years in between? They are treasured lodes of conflict, learning, growth, and loss, too.

"Such a sleep they sleep,
those men I loved."

You are Church, with or without anybody. And where I go it is in your name and The Name I learned to say better while among you. I shall be close enough to hear of and rejoice in the children. My constant love is to them—as to you.

I rejoice now in this strange new turn for which all my life has prepared me. But if any ever preaches any other gospel to you, "let him be anathema".

In Love,
CARLYLE MARNEY

Bob Bryant says of Marney,

I believe Marney brought on his heart attack. He kept long hours, often came in at two in the morning. And people from the church showed up at his house at 2 A. M. He read late, then got up early to write. Even after he left the church and would come back to our house, people kept pestering him still.

During his ministry here, Marney may have gone through a period where he was afraid to let people know he loved them. Many people tried to get close to him and he wouldn't allow it, couldn't afford it. After his illness, he found out he could let them love him and let them know.

Marney had lung surgery not long after his heart attack. I came to the hospital room, I don't know why they let me in, just as they wheeled Marney in, tubes in his chest, half cut open. Marney there sitting on the edge of his bed hurting awful, said to me, "I hope like hell this is not a professional call."

The first time he came back from Interpreters' House after his illness, he hugged me. It was the shock of my life. I said to him, "I like that." From then on, it was a hugging relationship. Our relationship became more personal after he left here than when he was here. Much deeper.

After Marney had left Myers Park, I was to meet him for church one Sunday. I saw him driving round the block four times. I knew it wasn't because he couldn't find a parking place. Marney never got over missing the pulpit, particularly this one. It was very, very difficult for him to sit in this church. That day we sat in the last row. During the final hymn, as it began, he said, "let's go." But he was all right at Gene Owens' installation and Bruce Page's ordination.

Marney let me read his manuscript for his last book before it was finished. I think he wanted to have people understand what he thought the Christian message to be.

I recall his talking about "times of interminable silence," and I also remember a phrase of his, "every man reaches a point where he realizes he's done all he's going to do."

After he left us following his heart attack, he had these times of depression. His was a massive ego, and after he left here, it didn't get tended to.

STORIES

There are some individual stories of continuing relationship with Marney that defy a category or any further editing. No story is typical. Nor any relationship. Some are disarmingly candid. Others were withheld, not given at all; the reason, as one put it, they were "sacred stories" and remain so.

But during the generous conversations, in many of them, consistently a fragile, unusual element was present. Was it imagination, the listener's propensity for belief, or was there something quite remarkable in what is remembered?

Ann Phillips . . .

One Sunday afternoon we had come in from the swimming pool and while I was putting the baby to bed, Jeffrey, our two and a half year old, scooted out next door in his wet bathing suit. He looked in the mail slot to see if Mrs. Marney was home. He walked in the door, went upstairs, and crawled in the bed with Dr. Marney who was taking a nap. Jeffrey felt he had a special place there. He would go over and sew with Mrs. Marney. She had lost several children and had two girls.

Once when I was walking across the yard, Marney came out and said to me that I was filling roles in my family that really weren't mine. I was in my twenties then. My younger sister came and would spend a lot of time with me and I guess Marney saw she couldn't get along with mother. She lived with me at least one summer. I got her in camp or schools. Marney noticed this and he would really throw things at me like a ball. Like you must love yourself to love others. I think probably I had never been encouraged as a child to feel as good about myself as I should have. He saw these things.

When friends in Marney's church would say that he just didn't like women, I just didn't think this was true at all. Maybe there were just some people that he was more on a wave length with than others. I probably saw parts of him that other people didn't see. One Saturday afternoon the children and I were walking up toward the church and he walked with us talking about how much the business of the church bored him, that they had to hire someone to take care of the big business that does go on in all churches.

I also remember hearing him say how much people like Rush Dickson and Frank Dowd and Guy Carswell meant to him. How much he really loved them. And this is a very rare thing to hear a big man say that he really loved another man.

I saw him as a many faceted person. I don't think he belonged in any religion. When I heard that a Baptist minister was moving next door, I wasn't sure that I was going to like it. But I found that his feeling for religion and life was so totally universal. Many people had no idea what he was saying. He lived above and beyond his time. And yet in his time.

Probably a lot more is written on my face that I don't see. He probably looked more, looked behind it or maybe cared or took time. And yet I was just busy hanging out diapers and taking children for walks and all the neighbor children and dogs would go along with me.

I felt Marney was very approachable. Yet I heard people, one friend, say she didn't think he was approachable at all. I think he took a drink too which always made me laugh because I thought, "Oh, won't some of them think that he is going to go to hell because he took a drink." Of course, I've had very bad experiences in my own family with drinking. But I think drinking is just like everything else in life. It is how you handle it.

I know it worried Mrs. Marney that he would go down to meet anybody who needed him at any hour. They would call and he would meet them in the back streets of Charlotte if that's where they called from. You would see that big Jeepy sort of car that he drove around going up Providence Road toward Presbyterian or Memorial hospitals. I think maybe one reason he had to leave Charlotte was because he couldn't do anything halfway.

All these people who need to be listened to, maybe for Marney that was the ministry. Even though, when I knew him, I didn't feel that I could say very much. I wouldn't go to him and it is just what he would perceive in casual conversation. When he told me I was taking too many roles in my family, I remember thinking I'm taking the load of these people. I was allowing them to use me. I realize this, but I think it is probably a great compliment to be used and giving and helping.

Haynes Baird . . .

The way I best remember him is that Marney and I were so much alike. He used to say we were both just as bullheaded as hell.

I got to know him as well as I did since I'm an individualist who might be my worst enemy by expressing things because dogmatism and ignorance are so close akin. But Marney and I were so expressive. We said what we thought, agreed or disagreed. I asked him about something and it started an argument.

After he died I got a note from Elizabeth saying she remembered "those midnight and after midnight sessions you and Marney had when we lived out there on Providence Road." He might call me up at 9 or 10 o'clock at night and say, "What are you doing?" And I'd say "I'm in bed. Asleep. What do you mean by waking me up?" And he would say, "Oh hell, go on and sleep and forget it." Or if I were not doing anything he would say, "Do you want to talk a little bit" about something or other? And I would say, "Yeah," and I'd run by there and we would go out and get a cup of coffee. At that time I smoked. Maybe I was chewing, then I stopped smoking and went to chewing, trying to wean myself off cigarettes. He said, "Anyway you're level-headed, it runs down each corner of your mouth equidistant."

Sometimes we might talk about the black situation. Or I wrote a term paper one time on the proof or disproof of an omnipotent ruler. We got on that. How do you know there's a God? What's after this life? What happens to you when you die? Something like that. It could be anything and we might disagree violently about it. He said, "You know, at times I might accuse you of being two-faced except if you had a better face, you'd wear it."

And he might meet my wife at church one day and say, "Where is that lousy so-and-so? I know, and don't tell me he is tired. He just wanted to sleep today." You know, that was just Marney. I'm sure that had we been a man and a woman with dispositions like his and mine, we could never have lived in the same house.

We argued about integration and, of course, Billy Graham. He and I disagreed on that too.

Marney had the bigger issues at heart and maybe I'd be talking smaller issues. The issues might be many things. Cigarettes for one. He smoked just like I did. His was a nervous thing, a compulsive thing. I think they may have hastened his cornonary. He was that Type A personality, that driving intellectual individual. Like a caldron, he was boiling inside all the time.

He never impressed me as being egotistical. . . . We all want to feel important. I think that's true of everybody who amounts to anything. An individual whom I would term egotistical is one who was interested in doing almost anything to boost themselves up. Marney was everything in the world but that. He would be almost the reverse at times because he might just out with what he thought, "No, by God, I don't think that is right at all" to somebody that he might be asking for money for the church.

If he ever accomplished a great deal as a community conscience I am unaware of it. Marney was not the political type to see ideas of that nature. Now I think that people who bought his ideas bought them because they were great ideas, not because he led them like a politician would lead masses of people to get worked up. I think Billy Graham could sell ice boxes to Eskimos. Marney, I don't think, if he didn't believe in it, could sell you a ten dollar bill for two cents.

I believe I know why Marney came to Myers Park Baptist Church. He thought that here is a bunch of rich people who are going to hell on wheels as fast as they can and maybe I can get down there and have something to do with saving them. That's exactly the reason I think he came, from our conversations. He was certainly in a church down there [in Texas] that was much bigger and probably much wealthier and politically more powerful.

I never did get around to asking him whether he thought he had helped save them or not. It just didn't dawn on me that Marney would have a heart attack. You know you let time run out on you. You never get around to all these things.

The question of what happens when you die worried Marney as much as anything else. He was in constant search for the answer to that question.

Marney talked about hunting, but he didn't like to hunt. He was always saying, "Haynes, I want to go hunting with you." He found out that I hunted down at so-called Dabbs Crossroads. Jim Dabbs was one of the great pioneer leaders of the south, wrote books on integration, was ostracized in South Carolina. After Marney found out I hunted down there and visited Jim Dabbs' home, that's why he kept talking to me a lot about hunting. I don't believe he would have shot a bird if he tried.

He had Irish setters and loved dogs, but he never went hunting with me even though I called him several times. He was a little chicken-hearted when it came to anything dying.

I guess one reason Marney meant a lot to me was where we both grew up. He grew up in eastern Tennessee and I grew up in western North Carolina, just as poor as Job's turkey moneywise. We had that in common and the Depression. When he called up at night to say, "What are you doing?" we never lacked a topic. We never talked much about religion. I guess our relationship just wasn't one for me to try to educate him about any aspect of medicine or him to educate me about religion. It was just sort of a mutual enjoyment of getting the ideas of two people who pursue a different line.

He'd say to me, "Haynes, you're so countrified, you're slew-footed."

He was such a complex man with a mind as he had, to understand it almost in a way reminded me of looking in the cockpit of an airplane. All those different lights and gadgets and everything. To listen to him talk about some of the things he thought, I just didn't understand it. It was too far above me and my thinking just doesn't take it in. I've often thought that it might have been in a way a detriment as far as his preaching was concerned.

I used to say, "Marney, you know, you are an excellent preacher, but you just ain't worth a damn as a pastor." He would say, "What do you mean by that?"

"You've got to lead these people. Get them to do the right thing."

He would say, "What do you think I'm doing, or trying to do?" We would argue the difference in a preacher and a pastor, a shepherd leading the sheep rather than a preacher who preaches on Sunday and goes to the middle of the week with a message to get across here and there, all over the country. He would say, "What do you think I'm running all over the country for? What do you think I'm trying to do? Do you think I'm spinning my wheels?"

Yes, we enjoyed each other.

Reverend Charlie Milford,

We were at the State Baptist Convention in Greensboro and several of us were not too enthusiastic about the convention anyway, but we were there and were trying to be serious about it. We went in to hear the President's address. The President rose and, as he did, he said, "Brethren, I stand before you clothed in robes of humility." I turned and looked at Marney and he looked at someone on the other side of him and the three or four of us got up and walked out. We were near the back so there really wasn't any disturbance.

We went next door to a little coffee shop and that morning Marney began "the Humility Club," a group of Baptist ministers who were humble enough to be proud of it. We determined that we couldn't sit and listen to that brother talk about his humility, that we could share ours with each other. We were quite certain that we were much more humble than he was.

Marney was my teacher, pastor, and very dear friend. Our friendship never involved a great deal of time. The weekly meeting of the Humility Club was the major time that I was with him, I suppose.

One of the Friday mornings I was deeply depressed and I cannot remember for the life of me what it was, but I know that I went in that morning and sat down at the table while several others were already there. They were over at the coffee pot carrying on the usual, lighthearted conversation and foolishness that we so often shared. But I just sat down by myself. I was very burdened and Marney came in and, perceptive as always, instead of going immediately to the group that was laughing and talking and enjoying their coffee as I'm sure he would have liked to do, immediately sat down across the table from me and didn't say a word. He didn't make a sound. He just sat there for a moment until I looked up and said, "Marney, do you really believe, do you really believe, that almighty God can forgive anything?"

He leaned forward across the table and said, "I forgive you." You know how he could do it. I wish I could imitate him. "I forgive you." Not God forgives you, but I forgive you and then he got up and joined the group. It was an experience that I have never known before or since.

And other times, the teaching. A combination of gracing and teaching. It was about a year before he published THE COMING FAITH. He came in that morning for the seminar. All of us were gathered. We tried to get there before he did and when he walked into the room, it almost looked like he was walking about six feet or four feet at least off the floor. He was just walking on air. He couldn't wait to get started; to tell us what he had discovered in the Book of Romans, in terms of its universal nature, the universal quality of Christ, his "Your name is Jesus" discovery that Adam is not primary, but Christ is primary and Adam is secondary. From the fifth, sixth and seventh Chapters of Romans we heard that morning in rough form the discovery that later on became polished in THE COMING FAITH. He was so excited about it. The night before he had worked until ten or eleven o'clock and slept until three or four and got up to go back to work and had come directly from his study then to our seminar at ten. I would have been utterly exhausted at that point. He was so exhilarated that one has to be reminded of the time when Jesus at the well in Samaria told the desciples that he had meat to eat that they knew not of. He confessed his indulgence in excessive work. Marney's theological lust, as he often called it, may have shortened his life. I don't know. But for sure he did not shorten his living, because he lived more than he could have lived had he not been so exhilarated by what he was doing.

To be with him there on Wolf Pen Mountain and walk, or on occasion ride in his four wheel drive vehicle, up toward the top of that mountain. To walk the rest of the way and simply sense his joy in the forest and the mountains and being outdoors. There was something about him in these times that you couldn't really describe.

When our people would go to Interpreters' House for the week-end retreats, as we did I think three or four times, I thought it was absolutely unreasonable that he and Elizabeth would invite the entire group over to his house on Saturday evening after supper and we would have wine and cheese or apples or something and sit around in the apple house study there. Such a unique place that it was an exceedingly good thing for these of our people who had never seen him in these circumstances to be with him there. Usually the seminar would not amount to much that night, because the room is not adequate for everyone to see and talk. It's too broken up, but the experience was worth more. One year when we were there, T. J. Reddy read some of his poetry for us and convinced us emotionally what some want to confront intellectually that this man was too sensitive, and as Marney said, could not kill, not comfortably kill, an insect, much less there was no way he could have participated directly in killing a horse.

One other memory that stands out so dramatically goes way back. He invited a group of about fifty ministers to come up to an Inn or Motel in Maggie Valley. That was the first time I ever heard him, and I suspect it was one of the first times that he used or began to use the technique that became so important at Interpreters' House. After supper he gathered all that group of ministers in that dining room, a widely diverse group from all over the country, and with all kinds of persuasions. I don't know how I happened to be there, but I'm glad that I was. I can remember that I was sitting directly across the table from Martin England, and Marney began with his technique of "How is it with you?" Or "How is it where you are at?"

That's what he would say. And it didn't work that night at first. Some people gave some superficial answers. Some brother talked about the difficulty of raising the budget at his church. And it must have been a pretty heavy toll on Marney to be polite, but he was that night. I've heard him when he wasn't, and thought he was right not to be. But he just accepted that and said, "Yes, that's an important thing" and went on. What makes it stand out in my memory is that when nobody else said anything, I (being almost frightfully bashful and reticent at times and yet brashly arrogant at others) was burdened. The concern was yet to be answered in THE COMING FAITH *and* THE CARPENTER'S SON, *so finally when nobody said anything, and it was quiet for a ways I said, "Well, I don't want anybody to laugh, but what I want to know is who is Christ?"*

I remember that there was almost a shocked silence. I didn't know what that meant until Martin England, sitting across the table, very graciously said, "Nobody is going to laugh. We all would like to know." For me the answer came in THE CARPENTER'S SON *and* THE COMING FAITH *and in many other subsequent conversations.*

Marney turned me loose. Marney freed me to go where I wanted to go, where I wanted to be. It was in that sense that he had his greatest influence.

I suspect that I never would have discovered without his telling me that the incarnation is real. I really didn't think it was real until Marney made it real. You see the traditional Southern Baptist doesn't believe in the incarnation. They believe that Jesus is God. That's not incarnate. Jesus is man. And uniquely man, but man and to be human is the ultimate.

This turned me loose to be freed to go anywhere the truth lies without any fear. I used to be so afraid of hurting people. I was afraid to preach the truth because I was afraid people would hear error, that it would destroy their faith. Marney convinced me that the people were competent. The most important way that he did it was in his believing in my competence.

I remember when he had his chest surgery. I don't know why, but it thrilled me that he sent for me. There wasn't anybody allowed to see him except his doctor and a few people who were special and he sent for me. I couldn't believe it, but I went as fast as I could go. He was lying up there in that bed buck naked with a sheet thrown over a little bit of him and practically rolling in the bed, just turning constantly. It was two days after his surgery. "Charles, there are three things that I know that you don't know."

I said, "What's that, Marney?"

He said, "I know I do not have lung cancer. I know that I can face death without fear. You don't know that. And I know that I can suffer God-awful pain and not lose my sense of humor. You don't know that."

He kept turning and turning and I asked, "Why are you turning so much?"

He said, "The damn doctor said if I turned and moved I would get well quicker. I figure the more I turn the quicker I will get well."

One other time I asked Marney, "What do you do when you finish preaching your Sunday sermon and you know what you said wasn't true"

"Was it true when you said it?"

"Yes, but then later I wondered."

"All the truth you can ever have is in moments. At the moment it was true."

Yes, I did love Marney. I do love him. He lives right on.

Diannah Ellis . . .

I first heard Marney the spring of my freshman year at college in 1959, at the BSU convention in Charleston where Marney was the keynote speaker. I didn't know anybody, but there was a big impression on me. I was beginning to question my faith. Marney in his lectures came on personably and caring. I had no personal conversation and was in no small group with him, but over the next few years we became friends at student gatherings. I can see Marney sitting with a group very informally talking, listening. We really mattered. When I think of college kids, I think perish the thought that I would be around them very much or spend any time really listening or caring about their questioning. What I experienced with Marney was a tremendous support of us as people in our struggle, never talking down to us, sharing a lot of himself and his theological "raps". He paid attention, took us seriously, yet he was always able to kid.

I was at Winthrop, but thank God for Clemson and BSU. When I was out of school and going back for mountain retreat on weekends, Marney and Elizabeth and Charlie Webster (in Marney's big old white Chrysler) Marney had to get the saddle out of the back seat and the dog blanket. It was the first time I had ever personally been with him and Elizabeth for any length of time for conversation. One of the first things I remember him talking about was his dog, an important animal to him, a big Irish Setter. I am an animal person and have had a lot of animals and it made an impression on me then, how much Marney cared. I had heard him tell his horse story before: we are like the horse way out in the pastures and the master comes to the fence and whistles and the horse pricks up his ears. He was using that analogy with man and God. The dog story made an impression (I've always thought Irish Setters are gorgeous, but I live in a neighborhood now with four Irish Setters and they are the hardest-headed animals I have ever seen. They will come to my yard, knock over my garbage can and when I go out to run them off, they stand there and bark in defiance). I think it is significant he had Irish Setters and loved them. There is just no training them.

After I finished school and was teaching in Gastonia a student of mine I was very fond of had run away and that was before kids ran away. He had been gone for about a week; it was very unusual. When he came back, his parents asked me if I would come over and if I would talk to him. I didn't know what to do for this kid and I didn't know anybody I thought would be able to hear him and help him. I thought he particularly needed some kind of male influence so I called Marney in Charlotte one day and told him the situation—that

Steve was really distressed. I asked him if he would be willing to spend some time with Steve. He told me to bring him on over that afternoon. We came over and I introduced Marney and Steve and I left. I guess Marney spent an hour or an hour and a half. He had never seen him before in his life.

Another experience with a young teenager was at Green Lake. The boy, Dave, was fourteen, so distressed. His grandmother was dying with cancer. He was asking me questions and I could share where I was but I felt uncomfortable with someone who was delving far deeper into the theological thing than I felt comfortable dealing with. I suggested that he talk to Marney. We made an appointment with Marney there at Green Lake. So many people were clamoring but Marney always seemed to have time. Later Marney remembered he said to Dave that week, "You know, son, you are talking to me like you are my peer? I'm old enough to be your granddaddy." And he said to me, "You know what that young man said to me? He said to me, 'Why, Dr. Marney, I never thought about it in terms of age, I just always thought about people talking to people' ". I think Marney loved boys and men, they had a particular attraction. My friend Ken Dean was Marney's protege in a lot of ways, rough, tough. He was head of Civil Rights in Mississippi, and poor! Marney met him when he was playing football at Carson-Newman. He would be an Irish Setter if I were going to make him an animal. But Marney loved him, bailed him out of more mess when he was in Seminary because he was always coming up against the authorities, I think he was sensitive to the struggles of men, the repression of men. I think men have been repressed in terms of socialization, of not expressing feelings. Marney was very aware, I think, of the whole being and the sexual dynamics of the person's make-up.

I did not join Marney's church right off. One day standing in the back of the narthex Marney said, "When the hell are you going to join this church, Champion?" That was my maiden name. He used to say, "You are a horse of a woman." I did join. I always felt a part of this church because of the care Marney showed me and everybody else in our orientation group. We mattered! I always felt this was my place. I did not ever work with Marney here. I attended and we came on Sunday nights for two years, but I was not on committees at that time. He met with the young adults every Sunday night for two years. He and Elizabeth would come. Elizabeth would do her knitting or needlepoint and contribute in her warm way.

At the time I was living in Gastonia and Art Ellis was living in South Carolina and we were going to be married at Myers Park Baptist Church in Charlotte. I don't know how long before your wedding you apply for your license, but Art and I had gone through what-

ever you go through and filled out the papers in Gastonia, thinking that you got a state marriage license. For the rehearsal Marney was out of town somewhere. A week later, Art and I were back from our Gatlinburg honeymoon. I got a phone call from my brother Jack. He said, "Diannah, I hate to tell you, but I just got a call from Banks McArver, the Register of Deeds, and you and Art aren't legally married." I said, "What do you mean, we aren't legally married?" Well, it turned out that you have to get a license in the county in which you are married. We got on the phone and called Marney. He said, "What do you mean? You call your lawyer and I'll call mine." He called Fred Helms. We called Marney back in a little while and he says, "You get yourselves up here. They could fine me two hundred damn dollars." So we met Marney in my house in Gastonia. He was on the way back to the mountains. My grandmother was there and my two brothers. He said, "Champion, I just wanted you to live in sin for awhile. I knew this all along. But you never have had much of a thrill at that." Then he said, "I now pronounce you man and wife in Gastonia, in Charlotte and anywhere you want to go." He always loved that story.

Art became important to him. I remember one time Marney was at Queens College, this was right after Art had just turned thirty, in November. Any time Marney was around I would go hear him and see him. I went and Art went the next day. Art was going through a lot of changes. Looking at his life, at what he wanted to accomplish. Marney got back to Interpreters' House the next day and evidently talked with Edna, because Art got a call from Edna Alsdurf that morning and she said, "Marney says come on up here." So Art went to Interpreters' House through the snow. Rode the bus. Stayed a week. Marney was picking up on the fact that Art was needful at that time, and his responding to us was significant. Art came back telling about the apple jack brandy.

When Karl Barth, the theologian, was going to be at Princeton there were going to be dialogues. The president of Princeton had invited Marney to come stay in his home and be with Barth. Evidently Marney was gone a good bit, away on week-end engagements. But, some of the deacons really sat down on Marney and said, "You know you are not going to be away any more for awhile." This was the story that I heard. Of course Barth was an important person to Marney. My experience was when Marney was here he pastored to the fullest. He was always accessable to me. Before I ever met Pris Upchurch, I was in the office waiting on him one day. She was on the phone and then Marney got on the phone. It was Pris Upchurch having a birthday party and they wanted Marney to stop by. His response, his warm and hearty response was, "Sure, I'll be by." And with children! He said, "I try never to pass a child without catching his eye."

I never picture Marney as larger than life. Marney was to me a human being. He could write and do all that eloquent stuff about humanism; but I knew it to be true through Marney. Marney was one of the first people who helped me to know how marvelous it is to be human; that we are not going to be perfect. That was one of his strong points. He had an intense awareness of God. He did not limit God and he did not limit life.

I would hear people say, "I didn't understand a word he said," or they would say, "Oh, God, I have to work so hard to understand." I never felt like I had to do that. Now I'm not saying that I could interpret, but somehow it did have to do with the splendor of life and with God and the struggles of human beings and those contradictions. Before I joined the church I came to some dialogue. He was saying, "Now, what makes the church different?" What is the church all about? We went through all the stuff—human, people and all of that. Well, that might be part of it, but Marney says, "You know, Jesus is Lord." I loved the Sunday he read T. S. Eliot's J. ALFRED PRUFROCK from the pulpit, all of it. It was magnificent.

I guess Marney was one of the first people that I really believed what he said. And it wasn't just his words, but his body language, tone of voice, humor, the way his mind worked, the way he caressed words, his struggle with his own demons. . . .

He was buried on July 5, 1978. I remember July 4th was significant to me because I had been involved with kids that day at the island campground at Huntington Beach, S. C. They had a parade around the campground and I was out on the beach about seven o'clock before the sun went down, talking with my friend Dolly Sue Pearce. Maggie, my ten year old, came and said, "Mama, I got a message for you." She was really uneasy and kind of giggled and then her face really went sober. And she came over toward me. She had the note in her hand and she said it's going to be hard for you. She just blurted out that Dr. Marney had died and then she hugged me. Art had been trying to get me since the night before and somehow the message didn't get through. Very significant that I had been sitting there and had just been talking in that quiet as the sun goes down—just really dusk—talking about what I was feeling in the terms of power and mystery of the ocean. Very powerful for me to learn of Marney's death at that moment.

I scurried about and found a plane to fly back the next morning. Also powerful was Maggie's awareness that something really important in my life, in other people's lives, had gone on.

SAYING GOODBYE

Rev. Bob McClernon at Memorial Service for Carlyle Marney, July 5, 1978:

I've had very little sleep in the past twenty-four hours, I have drunk too much, and smoked too much and I suppose that my present condition, if nothing else, qualifies me to grieve with you this morning. For I can imagine if I were there and Marney were here, he would have drunk too much and would have smoked too much. I think that Marney would be displeased if on this occasion I failed to quote at least one of those very important personages whom Marney frequently quoted, not including those times, of course, when Marney quoted himself.

Miguel de Unamuno wrote in A TRAGIC SENSE OF LIFE, 'A temple is where we go to cry in common. A temple is where we go to weep over the same thing.'

Certainly this temple is for more than crying. It is also for giving thanks, for praising God for his gracious gift to us and this world of our brother Marney.

Shall I thank God for a man who fought me gut to gut and mind to mind. Out-gunned me with learning and sometimes threatened to bury me beneath a mountain of books read. Blinded me with the explosion of ideas I scarcely dared to think and made me furious, so furious that I on occasion, and cribbing from one of his favorite stories, accused him of trying to slay me with the weapon with which Samson smote the Philistines.

I give thanks for a friend whose love of us and love of truth would not permit us to lollygag along on idealogical huff and bluff, sloppily thinking our way into some comforting and wholly illusionary never-never land.

I think that heaven has become a more stimulating dwelling place since this past Thursday morning. St. Peter and Gabriel and Michael and all angels had better have read Freud and Jung and Feuerbach and Tillich and Whitehead and Joe Carrington and Samuel Buchlender. Shall we thank God for a friend whose major vice, along with a host of minor ones, was thinking too highly of the actual and potential abilities and futures of his friends and his enemies?

Let us give thanks for Marney who saw in us, each one of us, what even now we are fearful of seeing in ourselves. Jesus who in the words of Marney's beloved Irenaeus became what we are that we might become who He is. Who called us out, prodded and pushed and coaxed and sometimes cussed us out until we began to believe the astounding truth, that God has not given us a spirit of timidity but a spirit of power and of love and of self-control.

Who will give thanks for a preacher in white buck shoes and a black string tie, no less? Mean enough and insightful and faithful enough to say to this church, this church mind you, of high upper-crust only made from slices of the apple of God's eye . . . say to this church, "Nowhere I have lived has there been such a great pressure to mash me into a perversion of the priesthood of the congregation. You would like for me, McClernon, Howard, Wilmot, Berry and the rest of us, you would like for us to be professionals, You would like for us to be hired priests." And then go on to say, "This congregation will let me be as gaudy as my ego will permit. The only real protection you people have got against my becoming some kind of pope is not your concern, it is my ego limit and the sharp minds of my brethern of the clergy and that is not much shelter."

Who will give thanks for such a salty tongue? Such an honest preacher. The congregation will give thanks. This blessed people whom he loved so profoundly and enduringly. Thank God for smoking lamp, shaking reed, wounded healer, pastor, priest Marney, whose barely concealed, half healed and sometimes open hurts and wounds were ours and ours were his. Marney wrestling with demons in the name of a God he sometimes felt had forsaken him. Marney fighting through sleepless nights at the ford of his own river Jabboch, Marney listening with Elijah through earthquake, wind and fire and hearing only that great nothingness, that thin sound of silence.

Is it any wonder that he could be our pastor and priest? Helping us name those voices from the past. Lived through our own dark nights of the soul. I thank God for Marney's tenderness. No man, believe me, no man could be more tender or gentle.

There was in him, despite all protestations to the contrary, a great deal of east Tennessee Baptist. Enough to make him haunted by Jesus and possessed by the God whose name he sometimes forgot and at other times believed he did not know. And for his final reliance upon Grace. Tenderness, piety, reliance upon grace, these in three paragraphs from a sermon he preached this past April. One of the last, I imagine, he was to write.

> *'If', he said, 'If entering now the zenith of my brief arc around and within creation I should enter God's grand hall tomorrow, called to my account for myself, I should offer this confession and defense if indeed I could do more than call down. But if able to give vocal response at all, I should say this, "Thou knowest, dear Lord of our lives,*

that for fifty of Thy/my years in ignorance, zest, zeal and sin I lived as if creation and I had no limit. I lived and wanted as if I had forever, without regard for time or wit or strength or need or limit or endurance and as if sleep were a heedless luxury and digestion an automatic process. But Thou, Oh Lord of real love did snatch my bit and ride me into Thy back pasture and didst rub my nose in my vulnerability and didst split my lungs into acquiesence and didst freeze my colon in grief loss and didst press me into that long depression at the anger I directed against myself. And Thou didst read over my shoulder my diary of that long journey when I did melt before Thee as mere preacher. Thou didst hear. Hear now my pitiable defense. In all my sixty years I killed no creature of Thine I did not need for food except for a few rattlesnakes, a turtle or two, two quail I left overlong in my coat and three geese poisoned on bad grain before I shot them in Nebraska, plus one wood duck in Korea. In all my years I consciously battered no child though my own claimed much need to forgive me. And consciously misused no person. Thou Knowest my aim to treat no human being as thing, never to hate overlong, to pass no child without catching his or her eye and my innermost wish to love as Thou doest love by seeing no shade of color or class. And Thou didst long ago hear my cry to let me go from Paducah. Thou knowest my covenant with Elizabeth in our youth and Thou knowest it has been better kept than my covenant with Thee and wilst Thou forgive? Indeed Thou hast. Hear now my intention with grace as if it were fact. I do and have intended to be responsible in creation by covenant and where I have defaulted do Thou forgive. Forgive Thou my vicarious responsibility for all the defection from Thy purpose of all Thy responsible creatures and accept Thou this my admission of utter dependence upon Thy mercy.'

'Naked I came into the world, how I am dressed at the conclusion makes no difference. A pair of jeans or a Glasgow robe, it makes no difference. Meantime, well I mow, I cut wood for winter, I clean drainage ditches, I preach what is happening and look to see what God will do in the earth. I watch out always for babies and little rabbits in front of my mower and old folks nearby and black snakes worth preserving, and little puppies on the road, and the young-old who stutter and laugh and can't hear, too. The cry of us all, 'Come Lord Jesus, come.'

PURE MARNEY

The following quotes come from Marney's interviews, sermons, books, newspaper articles, church newsletters, and hearsay.

Life never did lie down and behave for long, for anybody.[1]

* * * * * *

A man bets his life on the future of God, not his own.[2]

* * * * * *

If a man does not learn how to live in the meantime, he is less than half alive.[3]

* * * * * *

Humanism has always been my heresy. That some of my compeers have thought it stupid is no comfort to me.[4]

* * * * * *

Unanimity holds nothing together.[5]

* * * * * *

[About his two college age daughters] I enjoyed them so much it could not have been normal.[6]

* * * * * *

I'm not a refugee from a church that wasn't happening. I'm a burnt-out hulk from a church that was happening faster than I could keep up with it.[7]

* * * * * *

Twenty five years ago, I was more hopeful about the church as an organization than I am now [1967]. But I haven't abandoned the church. I never did stick with it as an end to anything; I stuck with it as a hoe, as a hammer. Church, bank, government, school—whatever—is not an end ever. It's a tool, a means to an end. And I have stayed with this hoe, this hammer, this shovel because 70 to 80 percent of the folk in the south are connected with it in some way.

* * * * * *

I don't know what made me go into the ministry. I had thought of forestry, that's what I really wanted. That's why I'm living here on this mountain, I guess. But I discovered, I suppose, that my gifts for books and people were at least as good as my gifts with trees.

* * * * * *

The minister worth his salt refuses to be hand-tamed by the gentry.

* * * * * *

A person who keeps Jesus too godlike doesn't have to be responsible as a human being.

* * * * * *

I hope to live long enough to see the Lord come to fix it, but I don't expect to. It is really up to us. God Almighty is not going to fix anything I've got the strength to fix.[8]

There is so little I can say for sure of God.[9]

* * * * * *

When Harry Golden says, "There is nothing in the modern church to offend," this is devastating, more than he may know. For "Offence" is a literal translation of what Paul says the Cross is. It is an offence, a trap to break your back, a skandalon, *a scandal to all who stand on its fringes—and the Church is no Church without this scandal, this offence, this Cross. It is Center. Nothing else must matter, too much.*[10]

* * * * * *

Truth can come up all around you like a covey of quail into which you have walked; it will flutter its wings and pound and fly away.[11]

* * * * * *

W. O. Carver was eighty-four years of age and still the great teacher when I sent him ten years of my struggle to understand the Church. He read it, and marked it, and sent back all 280 pages of it, scalded with his own concerns of more than sixty years, and said it would do. But then he added a line:

> *"Go on with your work," he said, "in a passionate evangelizing of this meaning of Church, but do not forget the bent knees and the loyal spirits of those who can never understand—"*[12]

* * * * * *

Most of us church folks are not responsibly free—we are just "sorta loose.' We hire a man to tell us that we are free and how we can keep this freedom. We expect him to tell us lots of things, but mostly we want him to tell us what to do in such a nice way that we don't have to do this or anything else.

But what if he himself does not know what we are to do? What if he just asks questions? What if he keeps claiming that answers have to come from congregations, not from pulpits? What if he keeps presenting the Gospel as a set of demands he cannot himself resolve? What if he keeps saying that preaching is a conversation most of which the congregation must contribute? And what if most of what he hears is a mutter?[13]

* * * * * *

The Church lives in the tension between the thrust of the fellowship of concern and the stance of those who simply cannot see the way. It lives in the tension between, loving both.[14]

* * * * * *

The churches of Charlotte don't have enough gas to get from here to Wadesboro.[15]

Herodotus claimed that the bitterest sorrow a man can know is to aspire to do much and achieve nothing. Not so; the bitterest sorrow is to aspire to do much and to do it, and then to discover it was not worth doing.[16]

* * * * * *

It is easy to tell when you are in a joyful church—its problems adjusted because its people are committed. . . . In our church I can find devotion, even sacrifice . . . unselfishness, service, comradeship and neighborliness—but what has happened to your Joy?

What brought you to such Joy before? What you were—and what you were giving to each other. . . .

Come, testify with me. It is the joy of a man who comes across an unexpected treasure. It is the joy of a man who receives a sought-after reward. It is the joy of a man in the company of his bride. It is the joy of a man who has found power within himself to do. It is the joy of a man who has something good to tell. It is the joy of a man on a venture, the joy of men not afraid of themselves, of time, or the journey, or its demands. . . .

The early Christians were absurdly happy and were always getting into trouble. This Joy—without it we cannot be. . . .

It is the joy of a man with his father. All little boys are bored by the same thing—that is, the separation, due to time, or place, or events from the thing or person they want. I always wanted Daddy to come home. I listened for the big whistle. I waited, I died until I could see his long legs moving through the trees in the park—and then the joy!

The church ought not to act as if its Father were away.[17]

* * * * * *

It's such a tragic thing when we become prisoners of our culture and worship such lesser gods. [In some communities Marney found] many gods, but in Charlotte, mostly one. A kind of economic god. Once he picked cotton and now he owns a mill.

* * * * * *

Without the will to do, we change nothing.[18]

* * * * * *

No one has ever talked of Peace and Hope with sense who did not talk against the backdrop of a great negation.

To be whole means to belong to a Community where there is something more-to-be than any adjective can contain.[19]

* * * * * *

[After Marney had been in Charlotte awhile] I've finally found out what a liberal Baptist church is. It's where two drinks are okay.[20]

* * * * * *

[Teenagers] really can tear your lives out. But they can't destroy them unless we have projected our own inner ego lacks into their lives for solution; unless we are using them to repay ourselves for our own deficiencies.[21]

* * * * * *

Sometimes it's a perfectly valid admission for a man to say God is not alive to him. But to knock Him off for the rest of the world seems to me presumptuous.[22]

* * * * * *

You'll never see a normal time, so get on with it and live in it the best you can. As in the day of Jeremiah, this is a time "out of joint," but you'll live all your life in a time out of joint. God is in our history even if it is out of joint.[23]

* * * * * *

Holy Scripture is the child of the believing community and not vice versa. It was remembering believers in community who put this down under the inspiration of the Holy Spirit. It was their experience with a living Lord that got in the pages of the Book. Unless we see this, we will not be saved from the kind of stupidity that is language literalism. The hope is that the believing community will still check its contemporary experience by what the church remembered was happening in other days. Authentically, the Bible will keep its precious place with me.[24]

* * * * * *

He was halfway up the broad entrance stairs to Marshall Field Museum and had stopped; hands on hips, socks drooping over shoetops, shirt-front bulging, campaign buttons on his lapels. With pens and pencils dripping from his pocket to declare his responsible status, he stood there. Arrogant in his ignorance I remember him because he was calling to a friend, "What's in there, anything worth my time?"

This is the question that the whole ill-gotten-up, arrogantly ignorant, busy-with-its-campaigns-and-cabbages-World asks halfway up the steps to Church, "What's in there—anything worth my time?"

And the questioner gets a variety of answers: "an easy touch is in there," says the professional transient; "a necessary superstition is in there," says an anthropologist who knows only that all cultures sport these quaint beliefs; "a fine political ally is in there," says Constantine, and most Emperors, and all Governors except the one who called the Little Rock Presbyterians names, not knowing he would need them.

What's in there? "A tie with our sacred past," says the ancestor worshipper, whether Shintoist or D.A.R. "A mighty fine preserver of the status quo is in there" says the social conservative who fears all changes. "The Church is a harmless and mildly beneficent carhartic" says a psychologist; "a convenient January or April charity," says the economic opportunist—by which he means that the Church is rather like a deserving old lady who is just a light degree of kin on one's Mother's side.

. . . From any angle one looks at the Church and asks "what's in there? Where is Center," the towering figure of Christ in Conflict answers us. Just as high on the hill over Rio de Janerio broods the sightless concrete Christus Redentor, so He looks down over the whole of the Church. From every angle He dominates—and in Him all the agonizing unanswered Old Testament questions are brought to resolution. Here, particularly, we see how the Holy God who is very far away can be very very near. Here we see how history is a matrix that contains both continuity and discontinuity, for God comes closer to us by interrupting history—by breakthrough—by crucifixion—by sharing our griefs. This Lord God of Abraham, Isaac, and Israel lets it be known here that He is God through this dominant exhibit: Christ in Conflict.[25]

* * * * * *

You can't crucify Messiah. Not so He stays that way.

But we have expected His cross to hold Him, and are thunderstruck when and if for a little He is inadvertently freed. . . .

We keep Him safely shut up in church. He was free in the streets.

We keep Him closed from commerce: but He was in the markets of men.

We put Him in a niche where He is worshipped: but He prefers our boats and our houses and our street corners and our Solomon's pool.

We force Him to peer through slatted apertures into tiny apartments; but what He wants is to be free to roam our whole dwelling.[26]

SOURCES

1. Sermon, "When Time Is Out of Joint."
2. Sermon, "Life After Loss".
3. Sermon, "In the Meantime".
4. THE RECOVERY OF THE PERSON, Abingdon, p. 32.
5. Interview, Bill Finger "Preaching the Gospel South of God," *Christian Century,* October 4, 1978.
6. Address to Parents' League, Charlotte Observer, November 9, 1965.
7. William Willimon, "A Prophet Leaves Us: Carlyle Marney," *Christian Century,* July 19, 1978.
8. Interview, Finger.
9. THE RECOVERY OF THE PERSON, p. 35.
10. Sermon, "In the Meantime".
11. BEGGARS IN VELVET, Abingdon, p. 41.
12. Sermon, "In the Meantime".
13. *Church News,* February 27, 1962.
14. *Church News,* July 10, 1962.
15. Editorial, Charlotte Observer, April 5, 1967.
16. STRUCTURES OF PREJUDICE, Abingdon, p. 14.
17. Sermon, "The Recovery of Joy."
18. Charlotte Observer, October 24, 1962.
19. Christmas Eve sermon, 1965.
20. Interview, T. J. Norman.
21. Charlotte Observer, November 9, 1965.
22. Charlotte Observer, February 20, 1966.
23. Charlotte Observer, May 26, 1969.
24. Interview, Lib Dowd.
25. Sermon, "The Recovery of Center".
26. Sermon, theological series, Charlotte Observer, March 27, 1966.

PHOTO CREDITS: The photographs on the inside front cover, inside back cover, and on page 62, are copyrighted property of THE CHARLOTTE NEWS. We are grateful for permission to reproduce them here.

BOOKS BY CARLYLE MARNEY

THESE THINGS REMAIN (sermons), 1953, Abingdon Press, New York, Nashville.

FAITH IN CONFLICT, 1957, Abingdon.

DANGEROUS FATHERS, PROBLEM MOTHERS, AND TERRIBLE TEENS, 1958, Abingdon.

BEGGARS IN VELVET, 1960, Abingdon.

ECCLESIOLOGY IN THE EARLY CHURCH, 1960, not published.

STRUCTURES OF PREJUDICE, 1961, Abingdon.

THE RECOVERY OF THE PERSON, 1963, Abingdon.

HE BECAME LIKE US, (sermons), 1964, Abingdon.

THE SUFFERING SERVANT, (sermons), 1965, Abingdon.

THE NEW BREED'S MAN, 1967, printed by the Ministers and Missionaries Benefit Board of the American Baptist Convention, 475 Riverside, New York.

THE CARPENTER'S SON, (sermons), 1967, Abingdon.

THE CRUCIBLE OF REDEMPTION, (sermons), 1968, Abingdon.

THE COMING FAITH, 1970, Abingdon.

PRIESTS TO EACH OTHER, 1974, Judson Press, Valley Forge, Pa.

Born July 8, 1916 in Harriman, Tennessee, Marney died July 5, 1978 at Lake Junaluska, North Carolina. He was a graduate of Carson-Newman College and received his Th.M. and his Th.D from Southern Baptist Theological Seminary.

During his ten years as pastor of the First Baptist Church, Austin, Texas, he also served as Professor of Christian Ethics at Austin Presbyterian Theological Seminary. Then after a decade at Myers Park Baptist, he moved to western North Carolina to found Interpreters' House, an ecumenical way station for ministers and lay persons.

Marney served as visiting Professor at Duke University Divinity School after 1972. During his lifetime he lectured and preached at all the major college, university, and seminary campuses in the country, served on the Study Committee for World Council of Churches, and was a Trustee for *Christian Century,* and Vice President-at-large of the National Council of Churches.

The generous assistance of the following persons made this book possible.

Edna Alsdurf
Dr. H. Haynes Baird
James A. Berry
Dr. Claude U. Broach
Stanford R. Brookshire
James R. Bryant, Jr.
Sarah Bryant
Alice Bryam
Dr. Sam Byuarm
A. B. Carroll, Jr.
Linda Christopher
Lake Dickson
R. Stuart Dickson
W. Carey Dowd
Lib Dowd
Ed Echerd
Diannah Ellis
Bill Finger
Harriett Fortenberry
Lillian Gardner
Kays Gary
Nancy Geer
Dr. Douglas Glasgow
Helen Goans
Arno Hart
Fred B. Helms
Ramelle Hobbs
Rev. Robert Howard
Vivian Jarrett
Dr. O. Hunter Jones
Amy Knott
E. F. Kratt
Connie Maccubbin
Elizabeth Marney
Lex Marsh
Rev. Robert McClernon
Rev. Charles Milford
Rolfe Neill
T. J. Norman
Grace Phifer
Ann Phillips
William S. Pinson
Martha St. George
Sara Streeter Stowe
Charleen Swansea
Sydnor Thompson
Leslie Crutchfield Tompkins
Priscilla Upchurch
Bertha Wagster
John Wagster